SWING

Elite Leadership
for High Performance Teams

S I G V A L M. B E R G

WHITHORN PRESS

978-1-7373318-4-1

Dedicated to

Martha
Wife

Kristen, Suzanne, Sarah
Daughters

Ryan, Dave
Sons-in-Law

Sarah Kate, Sam, Caroline, Josh, Juliana, Katy
Grandchildren

Sigval (Sr), Ardith, Arden
Parents and Brother

Severn Leadership Group
The network of new leaders for America

Praise for Swing

"*Swing* is an outstanding contribution: the wisdom of its guidance, the articulate, concise, and compelling way you put the lessons across, its relevance to the current condition of the world, how you've managed to condense a lifetime of learning and experience into 150 telling pages. Well done indeed—if I may say so."
— Sir Adrian Montague CBE, Chairman,
　　Cadent Gas (UK)

Swing is a book that should be read, shared, and reread by every serious leader. This is a remarkable achievement."
— LtGen John Wissler, USMC Ret.

"It takes a unique person to write a leadership book like this. This book is a blueprint for leadership at every level, but I recommend it as essential reading for those who strive for elite leadership—the leadership of teams with exceptional missions."
— Geraldine Taber, Vice President, Small Molecule
　　Portfolio Group, Pharmaceutical Sciences, Pfizer

"With stories, case examples and considerable suggested action steps throughout, *Swing* spends most of its time—not telling us **to do** something differently but helping us with **how** to make these changes—how to grow into an elite leader. *Swing* is both remarkable and important."
— Hile Rutledge, President and Principal Consultant,
　　Otto Kroeger Associates

"A must read for anyone recognizing that it is the **team** that produces results, and an effective leader is the authentic **catalyst** behind such excellence."
— Alan Waltar, Past President, American Nuclear Society, Retired professor of nuclear engineering, Texas A&M University

"With *Swing*, Sig captures the essence of what it means to lead and serve teams and organizations with excellence for the greater good."
— Julie Campbell, CEO, Severn Leadership Group

"A must read for anyone serious about becoming an elite leader."
— Chan W. Park, MD, FAAEM, Director of Simulation Education, Durham Veterans Affairs Health Care Systems

Swing is the needed companion volume to *Network Power*. Berg describes the characteristics of catalytic leaders who are in the end the genuine difference makers in the world. This is a book that inspires all aspiring leaders to become their best in service to a noble cause.
— David John Seel, Jr., author of *Network Power: The Science of Making a Difference*

TABLE OF CONTENTS

APPLICATION

CONCLUSION

FORWARD

The evidence of a crisis of character and leadership is unmistakable and growing. This leadership crisis has contributed directly to plummeting levels of trust in the United States and around the world, with survey data showing diminishing trust in key institutions across society, including media, education, government, non-governmental organizations, and business.

The many failures of leadership in recent years have left us in a world where distrust is increasingly the default mindset. Tragically, this trust crisis, which has been years in the making, has been deepened by the global pandemic. At a time when we most need clear guidance based on trustworthy information, we contend with confusion and contradiction. We need sure-footed leadership yet endure its antithesis. The consequences have been profound, including mind-numbing human suffering and the continued erosion of trust. Today, we are as uncertain as we have ever been about which individuals and institutions are trustworthy. The crisis of trust is peculiarly damaging to democratic societies, which depend precisely on trust to enable representative self-government to function and to thrive.

While many of us may struggle with a sense of despair or even paralysis during such challenging moments, Sig Berg has quietly acted. He has planted seeds and has been cultivating. He has focused on growing and building. Sig has not been deterred by the current societal headwinds. He has been energized.

Sig is not a writer of books. He's a builder of people and of teams. He's a doer and a leader. But we can all be thankful that he wrote this book, mining and communicating deep wisdom about the heart of leadership. The challenges and inspiration Sig serves up could not be more needed or timely. If trust is at an all-time low, then the need for morally serious leadership is at an all-time high. *Swing* has arrived at just the right time.

This is a book about leading and teamwork. It's about purpose and service. It's about character and judgment. But at its core, it's about valuing people. Sig helps us to see that effective leadership is ultimately about caring the right way for others. It's grounded in a commitment to love your neighbor. And that kind of genuine caring produces trust, the kind of trust that enables us to accomplish hard things together.

Sig draws powerfully on one of the most remarkable exhibits of a team performance ever, from perhaps the most grueling of all team sports: competitive rowing. Weaving compelling insights from Daniel James Brown's inspired retelling of the story of the 1936 US Men's Rowing Eights at the Berlin Olympics, Sig explores what it really takes to be a high-performing team, and how to lead one.

This is not a simplistic leadership manual. It is a deeply insightful reflection on how we must get out of our own way as leaders, and embrace the character, mindset, and habits that define high-level, teamwork-producing leadership. Sig helps us see how a mindset that looks for quick fixes, techniques, or formulaic approaches is antithetical to becoming a leader who loves and serves. At the same time, *Swing* gets practical: why is feedback so important on a team, and how can you create a feedback culture? Why is micromanagement so destructive to team performance, and what is the alternative? Why is accountability so important and why can it be so elusive? What do healthy mentoring relationships look like?

Sig combines wisdom from his own experiences over five decades as a leader - in the nuclear field, in the Armed Forces, and in the public and private sectors - with up-close observations of leaders and teams. He holds out a treasure trove of wisdom for those who aspire to serve and lead well, drawing on a rich array of insights, from Clayton Christensen at Harvard Business School and Brené Brown of Ted Talk fame, to the proverbs of the Old Testament. He challenges our failure of imagination regarding the promise of teamwork, and helpfully guides us through a journey of leadership perspectives that offer a deeper, more compelling vision.

Sig writes as one who has been privileged to know that deep contentment, even joy, of leading and contributing to high-performing teams: teams where there is genuine trust, a shared understanding that it's not about the leader; rather, it's about the shared mission and how all grow and what is accomplished together. Sig inspires as he paints the vision of how selfless, highly collaborative teams seemingly leave the realm of prose for poetry. Sig both embodies personally and captures in these pages the paradox of how leading with a deeply thoughtful, intentional vision produces leaders who don't take themselves too seriously, leaders who can freely acknowledge their limits and help position their teammates to step up and contribute mightily, thereby leading a team to greater accomplishments.

I have been privileged to watch Sig as a leader who embodies the approach he affirms through his extraordinary work with the Severn Leadership Group (SLG). The SLG is a remarkable community of learning, mentoring, and equipping, all in pursuit of the vision of high-performing team leadership that Sig writes about in these pages. A few years ago, Sig convened leaders from various fields, united in their shared concerns about the leadership crisis and in their commitment to do something about it. The response from those craving a better way, rooted in genuinely caring for others, has been remarkable. From a small group first meeting in the shadow of the US Naval Academy to chapters of mentors and mentees around the county, the SLG is flourishing.

Sig and the SLG community have together embraced a vision of learning, serving, and leading that has produced noteworthy results, one day at a time, one person at a time, one team at a time. This growing team of learner-leaders, characterized by mutual respect is experiencing the reality of growing trust. The fires of team spiritedness and commitment to excellence are not growing dim within the ranks of the SLG. Together, they audaciously believe that our combined efforts can help make the future better than the present, and that we have a personal and moral obligation to make it so. May *Swing* help many of us catch the vision and be willing to climb into the boat. There's important work to be done—together.

Dan Bryant, *Senior Vice President of Global Public Policy, Fortune 10 Company, Former U.S. Assistant Attorney General, Co-chair, Wake Forest University Leadership and Character Program Advisory Council*

ACKNOWLEDGEMENTS

This book is about something I wish I had known years ago. Simply put, leadership begins with me but is not about me. It took me a long time to learn this simple concept.

Three aspects of my life converged to open my eyes. There was a renewed desire for more self-reflection and to pay more attention to constructive feedback. Over the years I have been on some great teams, some miserable teams, and often, something just called a team. In each situation, I was clearly a contributor to their performance. It was only after being on a team that performed at the highest level with a real sense of unity that I begin to sense in a visceral way that leadership was not about me. It was about a team–people, trust, and a common purpose. And finally, I have been blessed over the course of my life by having several of people willing to walk along with me and speak into my life. They listened, questioned, challenged, and encouraged me. While not always comprehending what they were trying to convey, their love and associated behaviors won the day! I am forever grateful for Gladys Ritchie, Bill and Trudy Nies, Jonas Segal, Dave Shugert, Fred Meuser, and Zack Pate. They were true mentors.

The work of the Severn Leadership Group (SLG) is to support, collaborate, and encourage the emergence of a network of a new kind of leader that seeks the greater good for all. I am grateful for the support and dedication of all those who are a part of this movement. The formation of the SLG has been a team effort. Ted and Anne Parker, Hal and Billie Chappelear, Matt Carr,

Bruce Viekman, Dave Brandt, Art Athens, John Allen, Ray Rottman, Dan Bryant, Dwight Holloway, Kathleen Morrison, John Bishop, Tom Nees, Dan Shipley, Jim Phillips, John McGaha, Judy Farrell, and Julie Campbell have all played a significant role in our development. Thank you all!

I greatly appreciate the work and collaboration of Hile Rutledge, President of OKA (Otto Kroeger Associates) in Fairfax Virginia. Your expertise in the use of Emotional Intelligence as an assessment tool has been vitally important. Thank you, Hile!

I am grateful for those who have given me strong encouragement in writing this book. It is based on the cohort workbook I have written for the SLG, Difference Makers. I must highlight the support of John Seel, the author of the book *Network Power: The Science of Making a Difference*. His advice, insight, help, and understanding have been invaluable. Thank you, John!

Without the love, support, encouragement, insight, and candid feedback from my wife, none of this would have been possible. She encouraged me to read, *Boys in the Boat*! Thank you, Martha!

Ora et Labora

NO LEADER LEADS ALONE

What mattered more than how hard a man rowed was how well everything he did in the boat harmonized with what the other fellows were doing. And a man couldn't harmonize with his crewmates unless he opened his heart to them. He had to care about his crew.

— Daniel James Brown

High-performance teams require a special kind of leader. This book is about how such leaders are developed. It is not about the leader, but the team or more precisely the leader in service to the team. Leadership begins with you, but it is not about you.

The purpose of this book is to reframe your thinking about leadership from an individual concept to a team experience. Such leadership begins with a virtue-driven person of character with a keen sense of emotional intelligence and is then integrated with the ability to harness the personalities, abilities, experiences of other people to serve something larger than any single person. Leadership seeks the ineffable: in rowing it's called "swing," that moment when divergent strength achieves the synchronized harmony of high performance. This is that moment when, to quote Aristotle, "a kind of a whole is beyond its parts." This is how experienced oarsmen describe swing:

Imagine that you are giving 110 percent effort to a task but because your fellow oarsmen are so much in synch that you can't feel any of their effort in any way that is different from yours. The result is feeling your own effort magnified by eight. The boat is moving powerfully but you can't differentiate between your effort and the effort of your teammates. The feeling is of power so much more than your own and it is amazing.

Swing is the goal of all high-performance teams—whether in a rowing shell, a submarine, or an organization. This book is about developing leadership in service to swing. Swing is different from winning. Swing is the experience of pure teamwork realized while enduring the extremities of individual pain.

Rowing is the ultimate team sport. In a racing eight, a 62-foot shell with eight oarsmen and one coxswain, eight powerfully fit individuals must harmonize the artistry of their stroke in a ballet of motion while individuals are experiencing their own individual hell. More than anything, rowing is mental resistance to pain while harmonizing one's performance to the others in the shell. The slightest deviation under race conditions can cause a disaster. There is no other sport that requires the sacrifice of self in service to the whole more than rowing. Legendary rowing coach and boat builder George Pocock said, "Rowing is perhaps the toughest of sports. Once the race starts, there are no time-outs, no substitutions. It calls upon the limits of human endurance. The coach must therefore impart the secrets of the special kind of endurance that comes from mind, heart, and body." The sport demands the most of every individual. Author

Daniel James Brown goes further, "No other sport demands and rewards the complete abandonment of the self the way that rowing does.... The team effort—the perfectly synchronized flow of muscle, oars, boat, and water; the single, whole, unified, and beautiful symphony that a crew in motion becomes—is all that matters. Not the individual, not the self." While demanding the most of every individual, it also demands the total synchronization of the individual effort to the other individuals at the point of greatest individual pain.

Swing only happens when all eight oarsmen are rowing in such perfect unison so that no single action by any one rower is out of sync with those of the other. Only then will the boat continue to run out fluidly and gracefully between the pulls of the oars. Swing is the elusive overdrive of rowing. It is most often spoken of in spiritual terms. George Pocock asks, "Where is the spiritual value of rowing? The losing of self entirely to the cooperative effort of the crew as a whole." The mystical and elusive ideal of swing is possible only when there is the kind of collaborative leadership that makes it possible.

Pocock learned leadership making and coaching racing shells. Others learn it around a boardroom table. I learned it at the foot of a nuclear reactor. Mistakes in this setting cost more than gold medals and quarterly revenue. Mistakes here can cost lives—something in the scope of Chernobyl. The setting for my education in leadership was as an executive at the Institute of Nuclear Power Operations, as the managing director of the World Association of Nuclear Operators, as the chief engineer on a nuclear-powered submarine, and as a parish pastor. I know the people at Three Mile Island, Chernobyl, and Fukushima. Discussions of leadership in these settings is deadly serious. High performance teamwork is essential. There are no casual do-overs.

So it was that I brought this same level of seriousness into my retirement. I could have quietly hung up my spurs, but I was haunted by the closing scene of Schindler's List. Oskar Schindler stands in the rail yard at his factory in Germany. His employees have gathered under the cover of darkness to say good-bye. In those final moments, he is given a letter signed by every employee thanking him for what he has done for them—saving them from the horrors of the Holocaust. Then he is presented with a gold ring. Inscribed in Hebrew, with these words from the Talmud: "Whoever saves one life, saves the world entire."

The meaning is unmistakable. When a person shows humanity to another, he demonstrates the continuing existence of humanity in society. Schindler began to weep and all he could say repeatedly, "I could have gotten more out. I didn't do enough."

As I look back on my own life, the story of Oskar Schindler strikes a chord in me. I, too, could have done so much more. I cannot change the past, but I can work at shaping the future. I also know that if I am to make any kind of impact for the common good, I cannot do it alone. And so it was the genesis of the Severn Leadership Group.

It is apparent to all observers of contemporary society that we have a crisis of virtuous, emotionally healthy leadership in service to the greater good. Prevarication, self-serving spin, verbal coarseness, and failure to assume responsibility, when not overt scandal, are too commonly the public traits of our leadership class. This touches the government, military, academy, business, and yes, even the church. My life is dedicated to raise up a new generation of special forces in humane leadership for the common good. This is the mission of the Severn Leadership Group: to seed organizations, governments, and institutions of global importance with virtuous, emotionally healthy selfless elite leaders. It is our conviction and experience that such leadership can be developed.

The purpose of this book is to explain how to do this. Reading this book will not produce such leaders, but it can serve as an onramp for a journey in preparation, instruction, mentorship, and implementation. To begin, there are certain attitudes that one must adopt. There is no personal transformation in a leader without a high degree of self-awareness. One must acknowledge the need to start on such a journey. In addition, one must strive to embody certain behaviors. True leadership is not based on values but virtues. It is not about matters of your own choosing, some form of value clarification, but rather aligning yourself to and embodying those enduring transcendent virtues that are rooted in the structures of reality. This includes developing a high level of emotional intelligence. Leadership is an art, not a science because its subject is people and, more specifically, people functioning as a team. It is about being held accountable in practice to those virtues within the push and pull of everyday life. Clearly, there is no such thing as abstract accountability. The mark of a leader is only seen in application within an actual organization or a given team. It is not something that can be learned from a book or in a classroom. Its measure is actual reality with people under pressure. The combination of attitude, attributes, accountability, and application serve as the grist mill for the transformation of a difference making leader. They change a leader's behavior.

Central in our journey together looms the figure of George Pocock. He is the legendary boat builder and rowing coach from the University of Washington. He serves as the philosophical Yoda of the rowing world. His insights on rowing serve as a direct metaphor on life. The story of nine Americans who won the gold medal at the 1936 Berlin Olympic games, a story told in Daniel James Brown's book, *Boys in the Boat*, serves as the metaphorical backdrop to this book. Pocock was a master team builder and the guru of swing. This concept serves as the master metaphor for this entire discussion about change making leadership. Where this differs from other discussions of leadership is that, in this approach, the individual leader necessarily fades into the centrality of the team. This is a book about leaders who serve high-performing teams, not a book about high-performing leaders.

A story from the 1936 Olympic gold medal race illustrates this point. Don Hume was the stroke seat in the University of Washington Olympic eight. In many ways, the stroke seat sets the terms for the entire boat. Everyone follows his pace and direction. In general, the stroke seat is someone with the highest level of fitness and the highest proficiency of rowing technique. In a race when the coxswain gives an order, it is the stroke seat who translates that order into the boat. The coxswain is a lightweight non-rowing person in charge of the boat, particularly its navigation and steering. Of Hume, Brown wrote, "He never seemed to tire, never showed pain, just kept going, kept driving forward no matter what, like a well-oiled locomotive." From his freshman year at

University, Hume was viewed as a sensation, perhaps Washington's best stroke since their legendary coach Al Ulbrickson himself rowed at that position. He was the son of a blue-collar lumber mill worker as well as being an accomplished pianist capable of playing swing tunes to Mendelssohn. Brown continues, "He seemed to have an innate, deep-seated sense of rhythm. But more than that, his mastery of his oar, his steady reliability, and his rock-solid sureness were so apparent that every other boy in the boat could sense them immediately and thus easily fall into synch with Hume regardless of water conditions or the state of the race. He was key."

During the Olympic eight-oar preliminaries, Don Hume was ill, running a fever with chest congestion. He had lost 14 pounds since coming to Germany. On the morning of the gold medal race, Don Hume's fever had again spiked. Coach Al Ulbrickson decided that he could not row now and alerted his alternate. The coach broke the news to the boys as they got up.

At breakfast they talked it over. They decided that Hume had to be with them no matter what. "They weren't just nine guys in a boat, they were a crew." They got up en masse and went to the coach. One oarsman said, "If you put him in the boat, Coach, we will pull him across the line. Just strap him in. He can just go along for the ride."

The weight of this decision is truly epic. Does an idealistic sense of team outweigh the liabilities of a seriously ill oarsman particularly sitting in the stroke seat? Does this sense of team outweigh an Olympic gold medal? Do the voices and sensibilities of the other oarsmen outweigh the considered judgment of the coach? When, if ever, has the notion that the whole is greater than the sum of the parts been put to a more thorough test? The University of Washington eight won the 1936 Olympic gold medal over a dominant German and Italian crew by .6 seconds. This book is about developing this kind of leader... and more importantly this kind of team. A team with swing. Leadership begins with you, but it is not about you.

Chapter One

PRECONDITIONS OF PILGRIMAGE

In a squad, you cannot have a crew without harmony. The men must like each other. There can't be any culls, there can't be any culls in the squad. The men have got to like each other. Eight hearts have to beat as one.

— George Pocock

Starting with the right attitude is key to becoming an effective leader. Cockiness is not a sign of leadership. Too many leaders think that their power comes from knowing all the answers or giving the impression that they do. Nothing could be further from the truth.

Most complaints filed to the U.S. Equal Employment Occupation Commission are against recently promoted leaders. The 2019 data shows that retaliation continues to be the most frequent charge filed with the agency, followed by disability, race, and sex. More interesting than the types of complaints waged are who they are primarily waged against. Most EEOC complaints are waged against first-level managers shortly after they have been promoted to this new level of leadership. They are against new leaders, not old leaders; those who have just arrived. Why might this be the case?

It exposes a fallacy in the minds of new leaders. Leadership is frequently thought of as an arrival. "I have finally made it to the corner office!" Leadership is not an arrival, but a departure. It is the invitation to begin an exploration or pilgrimage in learning about yourself and others. If you enter a position of leadership with the confidence that you have all the answers, that you know how to turn this organization around, that you are the apex of wisdom, the smartest person in the room, your leadership will have failed even before you have started. The power of leadership is vulnerability, humility, and returning authority. It is the opposite of a traditional imperial leadership style. The adage about it being lonely at the top is only a symptom of a hierarchy rather than a collaborative leadership pattern. Effective organizations have a team at the top, what in the Navy is referred to as the command triad or the "big three"—the Commanding Officer, Executive Officer, and Command Master Chief. Seth Godin expands on this when he warned,

> In an expert-run industrialized economy, there's a lot of pressure to be the one who's sure, the person with all the answers. Far more valuable is someone who has all the questions. The ability to figure out what hasn't been figured out and see what hasn't been seen is a significant advantage. Rarest of all is the person with the humility (and confidence) to realize that even the list of questions can remain elusive.

Leadership at its best is embarking on a personal pilgrimage of exploration and discovery. The ancient, Jewish poet captured this in the words of Psalm 84:5, "Blessed are those whose strength is in you, who have set their hearts on pilgrimage." If leadership is framed as a departure, then it means that it is essentially an invitation for growth and learning. A willingness to change, a posture of self-reflectiveness, and the openness for input are essential for effective leadership. This is the necessary starting attitude to becoming an effective leader. Ironically, it takes a strong leader—a leader with a strong sense of self-esteem—to know that he or she is not strong, does not have all the answers, and needs the help of others. Before a leader can be effective, a leader must have at their core this desire to grow, learn, and evolve as a person and a person in relationship to others. Essential is this shift from closed to open, from having all the answers to having all the questions, from going it alone to going with others, from a static to a dynamic posture. The call to leadership is the invitation to embark on a pilgrimage whereby you become the best possible version of yourself. Leadership is about change. Change that begins with you, transforms you, and permeates all with whom you come into contact. The first step in effective leadership is the willingness to be self-reflective, self-critical:

Who am I?
What am I all about?
Why do I behave as I do?

These are not easy questions. They are questions people tend to avoid, and they are questions that busyness tends to push to the backburner. Leadership is not about having it all figured out by yourself but knowing that you need others to become the best version of yourself. The first irony of leadership is that the way up is down.

There are no elite athletes who think that they can become the best version of themselves who do not have a coach. Having a mentor, coach, and advisor is not a sign of weakness but a foundational sign that you are ready for leadership, that you have adopted a posture of learning and growth. This is essential for you to become a person worthy of leadership. This is the internal gaze framed by the first question of personhood: "Who am I?"

Also essential is having the right external gaze. This second foundational principle answers the question, "What is my purpose?" Leadership generally involves assuming the responsibility for an organization. Leadership is thus often framed as furthering the organization's success whether measured in expanding its influence or increasing its revenue. What we decide is the ultimate purpose in our lives will frame our leadership decisions and our allocation choices of time and money. What should we focus on for effective leadership? Harvard Business School professor Clayton Christensen writes, "It is one thing to see into the foggy future with acuity and chart the course corrections that the company must make. But it's quite another to persuade employees who might not see the changes ahead to line up and work cooperatively to take the company in that new direction." The purpose of a leader is not identifying organizational goals, but animating performance in others, namely building up people. Put simply, the measure of a leader is their ability to build a team. The second irony of leadership is that it's not about the leader.

These two ironies are mutually reinforcing. When a leader is humble enough to know that he does not have all the answers and thereby adopts a collaborative leadership style, it makes it easier for the leader to allocate their resources around building a team. Leadership becomes more about listening than telling, people than spreadsheets.

There are lots of problems with quarterly or annual performance reviews as they are typically conducted. Typically, the criteria being used for evaluations are framed by the behavior and knowledge of the individual leader. What if this were completely changed?

Rather than technical competence, what if the leader's performance is based on his ability to build a cohesive and motivated team? If we put first things first, building up people and the cohesion of the team, then secondary things like sales, customer satisfaction, technical competence, and shareholder value will take care of themselves. However, this is not what is typically measured.

In rowing, when we focus on the athlete's 2K erg times, or the time of the shell under race conditions against other competitors—as important as these measures may be—we have failed to focus on the internal magical factor that makes all the difference: the relational dynamics between the oarsmen themselves, their sense of being a team. The true test of leadership is the ability to create this kind of alignment. This is the invisible culture that lifts the abilities of individuals to a sum that is greater than the parts. The measure of a leader is the ability to create a cohesive team with swing. Leadership is an art as much as a science.

Rowing is a very technical sport that easily attracts Type-A technical engineers. Consequently, there is math and statistics about every aspect of rowing. But there is more to rowing than its technical dimensions. Understanding this was the genius of George Pocock, who as a wooden boatbuilder combined marine engineering with the art of a craftsman. The task of building a fragile and delicately tuned racing shell has been aptly likened to the making of a fine violin. In fact, one of Pocock's boatbuilding team, Hilmer Lee, was a violin maker in his spare time. Pocock focused on the hearts and souls of his young oarsmen. He worked toward achieving this mystical emotional alignment between highly competitive individual men, each fighting each other for a seat in the boat.

Because Pocock was able to consistently create such alignment in racing shells, he became the "high priest" of the University of Washington rowing program. Years later, Washington oarsmen would remember that they always stood in his presence as his leadership came to symbolize this ineffable sacred thing. It is my goal for you to become just such a leader.

For such a leader, a combination of transcendent virtue and emotional intelligence are basic requirements. While this state in a rowing shell is a rare thing, it is not impossible to achieve when combined with a certain kind of leader. Such leaders can be developed. Such teams can be realized. Swing is possible. Required is a systems-based leadership approach that is grounded in three basic assumptions:

1. Leadership is defined by your character.
2. Character is shaped by timeless and transcendent virtues.
3. Selfless courage and servant leadership are learned behaviors.

Having the right attitude is essential. You must frame leadership as a departure, an adventure in change and learning, and you must recognize that leadership is not about the leader but the team. These are the prerequisites for pilgrimage. Leadership can be learned. This is where the learning begins.

Chapter Two

FACING IN THE RIGHT DIRECTION

The opposite of rowing is drifting.

— George Pocock

Rowing is one of the few sports where one looks backward to go forward. This is the way pre-industrial English river men rowed their boats. Boats are rowed backward because the muscle power in rowing comes from the big muscles in the legs, back, and shoulders. Steering the shell efficiently while looking backward is difficult, especially in head races with staggered starts rowed on a winding river. In these races, the crashes of oars and boats are not uncommon. Because a narrow 62-foot shell is hard to steer, it is imperative to set your sights in the right direction early in the process. Last-minute changes in direction are rarely effective.

Key Questions
The same can be said about effective leadership. Since leadership is not an arrival, but a departure, you need to know where you are planning to go. An effective leader needs to reflect early on how he or she will measure their life. What is a good life? How will I get there? Leadership demands having a clear destination and an internal moral compass to guide your decisions to get you there.

What is apparent to all older leaders is that you cannot achieve effective greatness by accident. It takes consciously determined self-reflection. Over the course of a life, it is the accumulation of small decisions that shape your life. A life does not usually consist of sharp turns and about-faces. Rather, it consists of undetected drift, the accumulation of a thousand little decisions. Novelist Annie Dillard writes, "How we spend our days is, of course, how we spend our lives." Her point? If you want to know what you will be like in twenty years, take a good look at the small decisions you are making today. Your life is the sum of your days. Tomorrow never comes. So, too, a race is the accumulation of a thousand separate strokes.

Likewise, your core convictions are not shaped by conscious life-and-death decisions, but by the small, seemingly inconsequential unconscious decisions you make every day. When our lives become a series of extenuating circumstances, an ongoing series of cheat days, one eventually realizes that your core principles have been abandoned for something else.

All effective leaders must answer these questions:

1. What is the good life? What are the metrics of success for your life?
2. How does one achieve the good life? Do you have an inner compass that will guide your daily choices?

Put more accurately, when looked backwards from the vantage of age and history, every leader's life is an eventual inevitable answering of these two questions. It is not a question of whether you will give an answer with your life, only whether you will be conscious of the choices you are making in time for it to make a difference. Are you rowing or drifting?

Too often we do not have a meaningful strategy for our lives. We might map out a career strategy for how to get ahead within a particular organization. But this is not a life strategy. It's running a race with blinders on. We may go fast but we will be off course. An effective leader must choose the right direction and be grounded in that direction with the right disciplines to get there. Hindsight is too late.

Swimming is a mandatory skill taught at the U.S. Naval Academy to midshipmen. Swimming wasn't something I did much growing up in Detroit. Now came my first test at the Academy. After swimming for what seemed like an eternity, I heard yelling, "Berg, Berg come back, come back!" I had gotten halfway across the pool and then somehow, I had taken a slow turn and headed out to sea.

When I returned, the instructor was waiting for me. "Your stroke looked pretty good, but where were you going? Were you swimming with your eyes closed?"

This experience taught me two valuable lessons. First, keep your eyes open and focus on the mark. If you don't, you will lose your way. Second, it is important to have people willing to call you back when you are off course.

The Relational Dynamic
This book follows in the template of the great examples of leadership who lived lives following the "golden rule," which calls leaders to love one another, serve others, and seek the common good. Harvard Business School professor Clayton Christensen warns, "MBA students

come to school thinking that a career in business means buying, selling, and investing in companies. That's unfortunate. Doing deals doesn't yield the deep rewards that come from building up people." The good life for an effective leader is not measured in dollars invested, but in individuals whose lives you've touched.

Followership and leadership are reciprocal relationships, each influencing the other. It is an interdependent dynamic of inspiration and trust.

Followership is a relationship of purpose. The leader and the followers are relationally committed to a common purpose. Each person has a role to play if the purpose is to be accomplished. He supports the leader by communicating what is working and what is not. The resulting relational culture breeds honesty, commitment, and trust throughout the organization.

Leadership is a relationship of influence. It is not a positional description—as a person with a position of responsibility may not be a leader. Likewise, a true leader may not have a positional responsibility. The leader's role is to see beyond the horizon, to challenge and shape outcomes while encouraging, teaching, and caring for those he or she leads. They are good listeners. They seek constructive feedback. They develop teams, not their careers. Leaders exist to serve their followers in service to a shared purpose. An effective leader is a difference maker.

Leaders and followers are relationally connected. Their dynamic is personal and collaborative. Ideally, they cannot function without one another. This dynamic will be explored further in Chapter Four as it is the key dynamic in effective leadership and is often overlooked.

First, leadership development begins by being a follower. Followership provides the opportunity for core virtues to be shaped, technical abilities to become proficient, work habits developed, giving, and receiving feedback learned, and teamwork realized. The foundational competencies necessary for a follower are the fundamental attributes required of a leader.

Second, leaders play a crucial role in developing followers. The behaviors of a leader influence the practices of the follower. Followers quickly learn if a leader is engaged or distant, practices what she preaches, sets high standards and holds people accountable, listens and shows empathy for others, receives, and provides constructive feedback, and is self-serving.

A leader builds the capacity of her followers. This entails teaching, encouraging, and developing the skills and abilities of each person in the organization. It's all about helping followers succeed now and in the future. In this environment, people feel valued and supported. It leads to an engaged workforce.

There is an ongoing dynamic relationship between leaders and followers. They are interconnected, relational systems.

The Inner Core
New York Times columnist David Brooks speaks of the difference between résumé virtues and obituary virtues. "The résumé virtues are the skills you bring to the marketplace. The eulogy virtues are the ones that are

talked about at your funeral—whether you were kind, brave, honest, or faithful. Were you capable of deep love?" We instinctively know that the obituary virtues are more important, but then everything in our professional and cultural life biases the other. We may believe that people matter most, but most of the incremental choices we make in life say otherwise.

These obituary virtues are closely tied to our moral core or character. They serve as a compass to guide the leader in their relational dynamics and organizational decisions overtime. Leadership development is a lifelong experience. It is incrementally transformational.

The heart of leadership is the revealed character of the leader, character shaped by virtues and beliefs imbedded in one's inner being. They serve as one's inner compass and in the end, direct actions, shape behavior, and shape your sphere of influence. The character of the leader determines the destination he or she will achieve. They are the leader's essential core. I believe that leadership is not defined by a particular style, skill set, or desired outcome. Rather, leadership is defined by one's moral core.

As human beings, each of us has a moral core. It is called our character. If that core is not protected, bad things will happen. When the winds of darkness blow, the heat of conflict sears, and every ounce of our strength is drained, how do we react? Do we under conditions of pressure and testing remain true to our core and the virtues that define it? Our core serves as our moral compass that guides us on the decisions we make on the journey to our destination.

Transcendent Virtues

There is a lot of talk these days about values. There is far less talk about virtues. Values are something that you choose and largely reflect your subjective opinion. Virtues, on the other hand, are transcendent objective realities to which you must submit. Values are like your choice of ice cream flavor; virtues are like submitting to gravity. Virtues are not optional or driven by opinion. Historic transcendent virtues are common to all cultures and most religious traditions. A commonly recognized and full flowering example of these virtues is seen in the historic life of Jesus of Nazareth. For effective team-oriented leadership, there are five virtues that are essential for character development: love, integrity, truth, excellence, and relationships (LITER). We will explore these virtues in more depth in the next chapter. Here I'll discuss further how virtues function in our lives.

Virtues are not revealed in abstractions, but in daily living. They are the guiding framework for the many small decisions we make each day. They are what keep us on track, in effect, stroke by stroke, as we head down the racecourse. Virtues are not something you make up or choose, rather they are something to which you submit and align yourself to throughout the race. While they are largely invisible, that is a person's character is not immediately seen, they are always revealed in your behavior and are therefore never fully hidden. Every life is guided by this hidden character. Your character is revealed in your behavior.

The question then is whether your character is fully aligned to those transcendent virtues that define effective leadership. It is not enough to know these virtues, being able to quickly rattle off the list of five virtues—love, integrity, truth, excellence, and relationships. What is necessary is to unconsciously embody these virtues through repeated practice and habituation. Neuroscience informs us that only about five percent of our choices are under our direct rational control at any one time. Most of our behaviors are shaped by our unconscious habituated beliefs and virtues. Consequently, three steps are involved in aligning ourselves to these transcendent virtues.

First, we must know what these virtues entail and have our imaginations shaped by the lives of notable exemplars. Second, we must practice these virtues during daily life. They are not learned from a book but embodied through daily living. And finally, as we are all inclined to rationalize our behavior and fail to see ourselves and our behaviors clearly, we need others to hold us accountable to the high standards that these transcendent virtues demand in daily life. All serious athletes need a coach to perform at their best, so, too, all serious leaders need a mentor who is aligned to these transcendent virtues to call them to the best version of themselves in practice.

To prepare to be an effective leader, we must have a teachable spirit and a willingness to change. We must recognize that the true destination of leadership is the empowering of others, the building of teams. To arrive at that destination, our daily decisions need to be shaped by transcendent core virtues. As these decisions are largely unconscious, we must seek to embody and habituate these virtues through repeated practice coupled with external accountability.

Swing in a team involves more than the harmony of external technique. It also involves the harmony of internal alignment to these invisible transcendent virtues.

It is not in the race plan prior to the race where the race is won, but in the consistent performance of every stroke during the race. Rowers may be facing backward, but when their destination is clear and their daily decisions aligned to a shared transcendent core, the shell moves forward with a strength of purpose and in an unwavering direction. These are the crews that exceed their individual capabilities and potential. These are the crews with swing. It is the opposite of drifting.

Chapter Three

THE INVISIBLE CORE

Building a boat was like religion. It wasn't
enough to master the technical details of it. You
had to give yourself up to it spiritually; you had
to surrender yourself absolutely to it. When you
were done and walked away from the boat, you
had to feel that you had left a piece of yourself
behind in it forever, a bit of your heart.

— George Pocock

There is more to a rower than what can be seen. This was
the mystery of Joe Rantz, the great rower on the 1936
Olympic team. University of Washington rowing varsity
coach Al Ulbrickson and freshman coach Tom Bolles
recognized that they had a problem with Rantz.

Ulbrickson had been studying Joe for a year now,
ever since Tom Bolles had first warned him that
the boy was touchy and uneven, that there were
days when he could row like quicksilver—so
smooth and fluid and powerful that he seemed a
part of the boat and his oar and the water all at
once—and days when he was downright lousy.
Since then, Ulbrickson had tried everything—he'd
scolded Joe, he'd encouraged him, he'd demoted
him, he'd repromoted him. But he wasn't any
closer to understanding the mystery of him. Now
Ulbrickson turned to Pocock for help.

Pocock invited the boy into his workshop where he was building wooden shells. He talked about the tools and the different characteristics of the wood used in the building of shells. "The wood, Pocock murmured, taught us about survival, about overcoming difficulty, about prevailing over adversity, but it also taught us something about the underlying reason for surviving in the first place. Something about infinite beauty, about undying grace, about things larger and greater than ourselves. 'Sure, I can make a boat,' he said, and then added, 'but only God can make a tree.'"

The building of the shell and the character of the wood became a metaphor for Joe's life. It was a strategic indirection that broke through Joe's defensive barriers that hid his internal turmoil and woundedness reflected in his deep insecurity, lack of acceptance, and inability to trust. Pocock concluded, "Rowing is like building a wooden shell. And a lot of life is like that too, the parts that really matter anyway. Do you know what I mean, Joe?"

Pocock was able to touch the mysterious inner rower. The moral core of the rower is the heartbeat of the crew. Ulbrickson was wise in taking the invisible core of Rantz seriously. He was wise to put his psychological guru, George Pocock, on to the task. Often overlooked by leaders, the invisible core of the leader ultimately makes the difference between average and superior performance in a team. You must attend to the moral core of your team and then protect it vigilantly.

Buried in every leader is an inner core. It is from this core that the life and effectiveness of the leader emerges. It may be mysterious, but it is the source of their mastery. Until

Rantz could overcome his inability to trust his fellow oarsmen in the boat, swing would remain elusive.

Over the years, I have served as a chief engineer on a nuclear submarine and later as the site director of a commercial nuclear power complex with two 1250 MW pressurized water reactors (PWR). As one who had overall responsibility for reactor operations, I also had the additional duty of being the reactor's conscience. I was to ensure that each reactor was properly operated, maintained and that people were well trained. My job was to protect the reactor core. If I did not, bad things would happen.

A leader's character is the leader's core. It must be developed, nurtured, and protected at all costs. One is not able to lead others well without the virtues of love, integrity, truth, excellence, and healthy relationships. These are the prerequisites for every leader and follower.

I describe these prerequisites in this way:

Love
- Serves others before self
- Seeks to inspire others
- Aims to build the capacity of others
- Believes in his team
- Displays empathy and compassion
- Treats others with respect
- Does not humiliate another person, group, or adversary
- Listens, asks questions
- Cares for her own personal well-being
- Willing to say, "No!"
- Can be tough or challenging when necessary

Integrity

- Says what is important and acts accordingly
- Aligns personal, family, and professional lives
- Doing the right thing when no one is watching
- Self-aware, self-controlled, outward-focused
- Willing to admit being wrong
- Appreciates personal feedback
- Pursues consistent behavior
- Humble

Truth

- Able to distinguish between what is right and what is wrong
- Recognizes the difference between fact and opinion
- Aware of who "I am" and who "I am not"
- Realistic about self, circumstances, conditions
- Willing to stand up for what is right
- Willing to speak up when something is wrong
- Honest

Excellence

- Strives daily to learn, grow, and improve
- Seeks behavior consistent with a life of character and integrity
- Builds the capacity and skills of others
- Brings the best out in people
- Sets high standards
- Holds people accountable
- Develops a positive and engaging work environment

Relationships
- Recognizes leadership is about people, not things
- Knows and cares about his or her people
- Listens, encourages, teaches
- Provides constructive feedback
- Focuses on people, not career
- Seeks the common good
- Builds trust
- Approachable

It is not accurate to see these virtues in isolation but integrated together. C.S. Lewis states that it is the virtue of courage that integrates all these other virtues at their point of testing. It takes courage to be a leader and follower. It takes courage to love others before the self. It takes courage to be a difference-maker.

Another way that these disparate virtues are integrated is around the positive concept of flourishing. Flourishing paves the way to authenticity as it comes from the ability to be both strong and weak at the same time. Flourishing forces us to face who we are. It requires us to embrace both our strength and weaknesses, our dreams and fears, and even life and death. Flourishing allows us to pursue greater authority and greater vulnerability at the same time. Flourishing occurs when rising authority and vulnerability are held in tension. Only when we embrace being both strong and weak can our true character emerge, enabling us to become the best version of ourselves.

Leadership starts with us, but it ends with others. If we are driven with a sense of who we are and what we are about, then there is a wholeness that gives us the courage to be a leader and a follower, confident and humble, demanding and empathetic, able to listen and able to give commands. An effective leader has drive, without being driven. Becoming a leader is a process, but it begins with being a follower.

The process of leadership development starts with the doable, for everyone is capable of being a follower. It begins with the ability to take an honest look at yourself, to acknowledge our own shortcomings and areas needing improvement. Leadership demands embracing the process of transformation. We might start with asking,

- Who am I?
- What is my purpose?
- What are my strengths and weaknesses?
- Where am I today and what are my dreams for tomorrow?
- Is there a better version of myself?
- Am I willing to change?

Individual Change Model

	Delusional Searching	Well-Being Pressing Forward
Timeless Virtues ↑	*Mentoring*	*Candid Feedback*
	Adrift In Denial	Struggling Frustrated, Discouraged
	Intervention	*Mentoring*

Self-Reflection, Authenticity →

There are two variables that are essential in this change model: the degree of self-reflection and the degree of alignment to the transcendent virtues. This sets up a four quadrant change model:

1. Adrift: low self-reflection / low virtue recognition.
2. Struggling: high self-reflection / low virtue recognition.
3. Delusional: low self-reflection / high virtue recognition; and
4. Well-being: high self-reflection / high virtue recognition.

The person who is adrift is not open to change and the timeless virtues play no role in their life. Their core is not well developed. Adrift and in denial, they do not know why, how, or what to change. Needed here is an outside intervention to break through the paralysis of inaction.

The person who is struggling wants to change but doesn't know where to begin. He is struggling, often frustrated, and discouraged. He knows why he needs to change but does not know how or which behaviors to change. Needed here is an outside mentor laced with an abundance of encouragement.

The person who is delusional recognizes the importance of the virtues but lacks any personal self-reflection. His aspirations do not match his behavior. He knows how to behave, but without self-reflection, doesn't adopt those behaviors. He is delusional about himself and the people he serves. Here, too, a mentor is beneficial.

The person who has well-being both desires change and is seeking to integrate the timeless virtues into his life. He knows both what needs to be done and is experiencing a degree of authenticity and purpose in his life.

Leadership begins by embracing this transformative process toward becoming your most authentic self in service to others. Here the leader is freed to flourish and knows that he or she has made a real difference in the lives of others. To this end, the leader protects the core.

There are certain attitudes that serve as preparation for effective leadership. In this introductory section we have examined four of them:

5. A leader must be teachable, open to learn, and willing to change. Leadership is the beginning of a journey of growth.

6. A leader must realize that leadership is mainly about people: serving, empowering, and encouraging them. This is especially so when leadership is measured by its ability to create an effective team.

7. To maintain a consistent people-oriented focus, a leader's incremental daily decisions need to be grounded in a steady commitment to certain transcendent virtues: love, integrity, truth, excellence, and relationships. Every effective team needs to be aligned together to these transcendent virtues.

8. Finally, leaders reveal their commitment in the daily practice of leadership not through some form of cognitive affirmation. It is only behaviors that matter. It is only behaviors that reveal your true core commitments. To stay on track, all leaders need an outside mentor or truth-teller to hold him or her accountable. In King Arthur's Roundtable, this was a function served by Merlin as the wise sage and Dragonet as the court jester. All leaders must consciously lean against groupthink in favor of celebrating contrarian input.

These are the attitudes that are needed as you embark on a pilgrimage of growth: humility, people-orientation, virtues, and accountability. A leader needs a desire to grow, a virtue established direction, and an unwavering destination in his sights. These are the attitudes that an effective leader must embody. Attitudes are internal to the leader. Attributes to which we now turn, are the objective characteristics of the leadership dynamic itself. Correct attitudes in the leader fuel effective leadership attributes in the organization.

Chapter Four

DIFFERENCE MAKER DYNAMIC

*From the moment the shell is launched, the
coxswain is the captain of the boat. He or she
must exert control, both physically and
psychologically, over everything that goes on in
the shell. Good coxes know their oarsmen inside
and out—their individual strengths and
vulnerabilities—and they know how to get the
most out of each man at any given moment. They
have the force of character to inspire exhausted
rowers to dig deeper and try harder, even when
all seems lost.... In short, a good coxswain is a
quarterback, a cheerleader, and a coach all in one.
He or she is a deep thinker, canny like a fox,
inspirational, and in many cases the toughest
person in the boat.*

— Daniel James Brown

There is a mystical relationship between leaders and
followers that is often overlooked. Discussions of
leadership that don't also include discussions of
followership miss the difference-maker dynamic.
Leadership is not a linear process that can be taken apart
into pieces. It is an ongoing synergistic dynamic that can
only be looked at correctly as a whole. We have looked at
it from the perspective of the attitudes of the individual

leader. We now look at the same from the perspective of the attributes that characterize an organization where effective leadership is present. Swing is a mystical, embodied, holistic concept and as we think about leadership, we must constantly keep this holistic concept and experience in mind. It is the whole that matters most, not the parts.

To put this in its sharpest focus, consider the relationship between the coxswain and the stroke. The coxswain gives the commands, establishes the stroke rate, but it is the stroke who translates the coxswain's words into action within the shell. To narrow this relationship to their functional roles is to miss the hidden dynamic that makes the difference. Jobs are to be done. Assignments are to be completed. Typically, the attitude is that leaders think and the hired hands do the work. Perhaps the traditional attitude muses, someday the follower can escape from the gulag and become a leader himself. This perspective describes the gulf between far too many leaders and their followers. This perspective does not create a high level of employee engagement or trust, leading to disillusionment and poor retention—resulting in mediocre performance.

This is not an attitude that will foster high performance teams or swing. To achieve this the relationship of the leader and the follower must be further explored.

The leader and the follower share a core commitment that galvanizes their identity, character, and behavior. They share a common mission, intent, or goal—why the group exists. Both the follower and the leader pursue the purpose with commitment and passion. Note, however, that at this level the dynamic is external and abstract whether winning a championship or exceeding quarterly sales goals.

For exceptional results to be achieved, the dynamic must shift from the abstract to the personal, namely the relational dynamic between the leader and the follower. The essential role of a leader is to inspire her followers. When that occurs, you can expect followers to develop higher levels of trust. The leader feels supported, and the organization sees improved levels of performance. The cycle then repeats itself. Over time, the process is reinforced, and it becomes self-sustaining. This mutually reinforcing relational dynamic based on mutual respect and affection serves as the flywheel within a high-performance team. An adversarial relationship at this significant organizational junction is a recipe for organizational disaster. In most organizations, however, it is the expected norm and the status quo.

Followership and leadership are defined in this way.

Followership is a relationship of purpose. The follower is a member of the team or organization focused on and committed to a common purpose. Each person has a role to play if the purpose is to be accomplished. The follower is inspired and energized to fulfill that role, knowing that any weak link in the chain could well lead to failure. He supports the leader by communicating what is working and what is not. A resulting atmosphere prevails that breeds honesty, commitment, and trust throughout the organization. At its best, it is a relationship of mutual affection. The follower is a key difference-maker.

Leadership is a relationship of influence. It is not a positional description. A person with a position of responsibility may not be a leader. Likewise, a leader may not always have a described position. Leadership is a variable of relational influence.

The leader's distinct role is to see beyond the horizon, to challenge and shape outcomes while encouraging, teaching, and caring for those in her charge. They are good listeners. They seek constructive feedback. Leaders develop teams, not careers. Leaders serve their followers. A leader too is a difference maker.

But what makes the difference is the conscious awareness that they are inseparably inter-connected. Leadership and followership are all about people and relationships. It is personal and collaborative. When successful, there is an attachment based on love. There is an awareness that one cannot succeed without one another.

This kind of leader is not born but must develop over time. We need time to create a sense of purpose, self-awareness, mutual understanding, and a sense of humility. The difference making dynamic is a mutual attachment between leaders and followers based on respect and love.

At the heart of this process is the development of core virtues. The virtues serve as a compass to guide them through life, particularly in those critical moments when a focused mind and thoughtful decisions are needed. One must do more than just think about these virtues, one must come to think with these virtues. It is in the dynamic of mutually thinking with them in a shared life together under pressure that respect, mutuality, and affection emerge into the difference maker dynamic.

All leadership development begins by being a good follower. Followership provides the opportunity for core virtues to be shaped, technical ability to become competent, solid work habits and standards developed, the ability to give and receive feedback fostered, and teamwork experienced. The foundational competencies necessary for a follower are the fundamental attributes required of a leader.

Leaders play a critical role in developing followers. A leader's behaviors are always in full view. Followers quickly learn if a leader is engaged or distant, practices what she preaches, sets high standards and holds people accountable, listens and shows empathy for others, receives, and provides constructive feedback, and is self-serving or not. The behaviors of a leader influence the practices of the follower. The imprint can be lifelong. Second, a leader builds the capacity of her followers. The entails teaching, encouraging, and developing the skills and abilities of each person on the team. It's all about helping followers succeed now and in the future. In this environment, people feel valued and supported. It leads to an engaged workforce as it is based on mutual attachment.

Leaders and followers do not work in isolation. They are an inter-connected system that is pivotal for team success. The dynamic between coxswain Bobby Moch and stroke Don Hume illustrates the difference maker dynamic under pressure.

In the 1936 Olympic eights race, stroke Don Hume rowed in the stroke seat even though very sick. Behind by a full five seconds, Bobby Moch pleaded with Hume to take the stroke higher. Nothing happened. Hume seemed completely out of it, his head rocking back and forth to the rhythm of the boat. Moch couldn't make eye contact with Hume. He fought off panic.

Daniel Brown picks up the play-by-play in *Boys in the Boat*,

> Bobby Moch was still desperately trying to figure out what to do. Hume still wasn't responding, as they approached the twelve-hundred-meter mark, the situation was becoming critical. The only option Moch had left, the only thing he could think of, was to hand the stroke off to Joe. It would be a dangerous move—unheard-of really—more likely than not to confuse everyone with an oar in his hand, to throw the rhythm of the boat into utter chaos. But Moch had lost his ability to regulate the pace of his boat, and that spelled certain doom....
>
> As Moch leaned forward to tell Joe to set the stroke and raise the rate, Don Hume's head snapped up, his eyes popped open, he clamps his mouth shut, and he looked Bobby Moch straight in the eyes. Moch, startled, locked his eyes with him and yelled, "Pick'er up! Pick'er up!" Hume picked up the pace.

There is a mystical connection of affection between the leader and the follower when inspiration merges with trust in a high-performing team. Moch and Hume went on to win by .6 seconds over Germany and Italy for the Olympic Gold medal. Leadership is about followership and followership is about leadership. This is the relational connection that moves teams. It is the difference maker dynamic.

Chapter Five

A PERSON TO FOLLOW

Pocock believed that rowing was the finest builder of character of any sport, involving as it does the most rigorous discipline, greatest endurance, intense concentration, and total self-control. He saw in it the basis for success in most areas of human endeavor—a willingness to pool one's strength in a common cause.

— Gordon Newell

A common adage in rowing is to, "keep one's head in the boat." This means in the thick of a close race, no oarsman should be looking at the competition or glancing outside of the boat. Rather one's full concentration at that moment needs to be on the rower in front of you. Any side glance will upset the rhythm to disastrous results.

Every great leader is somebody's disciple. You learn how to live from somebody else. It is a sign of maturity when you become aware of whom you have been following and can evaluate the results of their teaching. A person's character is shaped by their commitment to timeless transcendent virtues, which is further inspired by the life of someone who follows them. There is value in reading the biographies of great men and women. Upon choosing wisely, one must "keep one's head in the boat."

The leadership model of this book is based on character, a timeless and transcendent set of core virtues, and a passion to serve others before self. We turn now in the following chapters from the preparation for leadership to the principles required by it.

These principles are found in the writings of Greek philosophers and Roman statesmen (e.g., Plato, Sophocles, and Cicero), early Christian theologians (e.g., Augustine, Aquinas, and Erasmus), Enlightenment philosophers (e.g., Adam Smith, Jefferson, Madison, Thoreau), and modern-day writers such as James MacGregor Burns, Dietrich Bonhoeffer, Barbara Kellerman, Bill George, Ira Chaleff, Patrick Lencioni, and Robert Greenleaf. All emphasize the importance of embodying universal ethical principles.

Robert Greenleaf coined the phrase "servant leadership" in his 1970 essay, "The Servant as Leader." The servant leader is demonstrated by making sure that other people's highest priority needs are being served. Greenleaf writes, "The best test, and difficult to administer, is: do those served grow as persons? Do they, while being served, become healthier, wiser, freer, more autonomous, more likely themselves to become servants?"

Over the years qualities of servant leadership have been demonstrated in the lives of many individuals past and present; known and unknown. William Wilberforce, Mother Teresa, Nelson Mandela, Martin Luther King, Jr., Dalai Lama, Abraham Lincoln, Harriet Tubman, Dietrich Bonhoeffer, Helmut von Moltke, Raoul Wallenberg, Mahatma Gandhi, Albert Schweitzer, Ida B. Wells, Cesar Chavez, Oskar Schindler, Desmond Tutu,

and Thurgood Marshall—all lived lives in exemplary
service to others.

This aspiration of serving others is shared by all religious
traditions. All the major world religions—Buddhism,
Hinduism, Islam, Taoism, Judaism, and Christianity—
have versions of the Golden Rule. C.S. Lewis goes further
to state, "What is common to them all...is the doctrine of
objective value, the belief that certain attitudes are really
true, and others really false, to the kind of thing the
universe is and the kind of things we are." There are
timeless, transcendent virtues that are rooted like gravity.

My understanding of servant leadership demands five of
them: love, integrity, truth, excellence, and relationships.
It is to these five timeless transcendent virtues that we
now turn.

Love
The love of neighbors is shared by all major world
religions and exemplified by every noble leader. When
Jesus was asked what was the most important command,
he answered, "The most important of all the
commandments is this: 'The Lord Yahweh, our God, is
one! You are to love the Lord Yahweh, your God, with a
passionate heart, from the depths of our soul, with your
every thought, and will all your strength. This is the great
and supreme command. And the second is this: 'You must
love your neighbor in the same way you love yourself.' You
will never find a greater commandment than these" (Mark
12:29-31). Jesus made love the main thing both in terms
of belief and behavior.

When Jesus spoke of love, he was not talking about a
feeling, but a mindset, a lifestyle. He used the Greek word

agape to describe love. This word is about actions and behavior. Love in this sense is self-sacrificing, serving, and giving. It treats others as we would like to be treated. It walks the walk. In this Jesus is summarizing every major religion: "Do to others as you would have them do to you."

At an even deeper level, Jesus suggests that you become whatever you love. It becomes the controlling, determinative variable in your life. The question of love is not simply how you treat other people, but more profoundly what do you long for? The answer to this question will shape the lived arc of your life. Or put otherwise, your life arc will reveal your answer to this question. Are empathy, connection, and care for others the determinative longing of your life?

Rabbi Jonathan Sacks, the late British Orthodox Rabbi, and former Chief Rabbi of the United Hebrew Congregations of the Commonwealth, underscores the generative nature of love,

> The more friendship I share, the more I have. The more love I give, the more I possess. The best way to learn something is to teach it to others. The best way to have influence is to share it as widely as possible. These are the things that operate by the logic of multiplication not division, and they are precisely what is created and distributed in communities of faith: friendship, love, learning, and moral influence, along with those many other things which exist by virtue of being shared.

Jesus of Nazareth's life demonstrated the impact he had on others. His compassion, courage, character, and his ability to touch lives turned a small rag-tag group of followers into a worldwide force for good that has influenced generations. If leadership is defined as a "relationship of influence," or the ability to attract followers, then Jesus satisfied both criteria.

The virtue of love was central to the life of Jesus, but it did not exist in isolation. When one examines the life of Jesus, you also see the other four virtues: integrity, truth, excellence, and relationships.

Integrity

Integrity is living out what you claim to be important to you. Jesus' message was a call to live a life of integrity:

> The eye is the lamp of the body. So, if your eye is healthy, you whole body will be full of light, but if your eye is bad, your whole body will be full of darkness. If then the light in you is darkness, how great is the darkness! (Matthew)

> You are the salt of the earth, but if salt has lost its taste, how shall its saltiness be restored? It is no longer good for anything except to be thrown out and trampled under people's feet. (Matthew)

As a leader are you a purveyor of light or a dispenser of darkness? Are you salt that has lost all its taste? There is probably no greater basis for authenticity in your leadership than whether you walk the walk with consistency and integrity.

Truth

Jesus wanted people to examine themselves and the world around them. He called people to live their lives aligned with reality. He is much quoted, "You will know the truth, and the truth will set you free." The truth does not set one free in the sense of letting you live your life any way that you want. The freedom here is a life aligned to the reality that thereby enables it to flourish.

Do you know who you are and who you are not? Do you recognize not only your strengths but also your shortcomings? What shapes your worldview? Is it true? Are you blinded by your own ambitions, false hopes, or fictitious stories about the good life? What does the arc of your life look like? What do you leave in your wake? Are you shackled to the past or pulled forward by the future? When the storms of life come, and they always do, will the foundation of your life hold? Jesus warned,

> Everyone then who hears these words of mind *and does them* will be like a wise man who built his house on the rock. And the rains fell, and the floods came, and the winds blew and beat on the house, but it did not fall, because it had been founded on the rock. And everyone who hears these words of mind and *does not do them* will be like a foolish man who built his house on the sand. And the rain fell, and the floods came, and the winds blew and beat against the house, and it fell, and great was the fall of it. (Matthew)

An authentic life must be built on something. Is that something a firm foundation or merely shifting sand? Every life is a progressive visible answering of this question. For Jesus, truth is the only thing that will set you free.

Excellence

Do your daily behaviors reflect the virtues of love, integrity, and truth? William Wilberforce spent over forty years fighting for the abolition of slavery within England with his friends and colleagues. It was a lifelong struggle. Excellence is derived from practice. It is the fruit of a disciplined lifestyle and a consistent journey.

This journey of practicing and getting up again has a purpose—the pursuit of excellence. A person motivated by love and a seeker of truth realizes the inner need to change, learn, and grow. Excellence is a lifelong journey of becoming authentic: a person of character, behavior marked by integrity, and a calling marked by a clear sense of purpose. The goal is to become a difference-maker for the common good. As in most worthwhile journeys, the road is never easy. The legacy of your life, particularly in your relationships, is worth the effort.

Relationships

When a commitment to love, integrity, truth, and excellence are combined relationships become an inevitable priority. Jesus knew who he was. He understood his purpose and stated it boldly. In his hometown of Nazareth, he stood up and proclaimed the words of Isaiah as applying to himself.

> The Spirit of the Lord is upon me, because he has anointed me, to proclaim good news to the poor. He has sent me to proclaim liberty to the captives and recovering of sight to the blind, to set at liberty those who are oppressed, to proclaim the year of the Lord's favor. (Luke)

His life was focused on bringing "favor" or human flourishing to people. He called people to join him, spent time with them, showed them, held them accountable to be people of actionable compassion.

His ability to develop healthy relationships with people of varying backgrounds, beliefs, and perspectives— particularly those consciously marginalized by his society—empowered his leadership. He lived and worked with ordinary people and treated each of them with respect. Though he listened, he often responded by asking insightful, probing questions. When asked, "Who is my neighbor?" he answered, "Anyone you happen to come upon each day who has a specific need you can meet, particularly those others ignore."

Jesus gave definition to the virtues, he embodied the virtues of love, integrity, truth, excellence, and relationships. He was a beacon of decency, civility, goodness, a new day, and meaningful life. His presence made the lives of all around him better. He led from the front, but with humility. History has shown that such a life makes a difference.

Rabbi Sacks summarizes this.

> When then is society? It is where we set aside all considerations of wealth and power and value people for what they are and what they give. It is where Jew and Christian, Muslim and Hindu, Buddhist and Sikh can come together, bound by their commonalities, enlarged by their differences. It is where we join in civil conversation about the kind of society, we wish to create for the sake of our grandchildren not yet born. It is where we

share an overarching identity, a first language of citizenship, despite our different second languages of ethnicity or faith. It is where strangers can become friends. It is not a vehicle of salvation, but it is the most effective form yet devised for respectful coexistence. Society is the home we build together when we bring our several gifts to the common good.

Servant leadership is the foundation for authentic leadership—upon which everything else is built. It is not about a style of leadership but becoming the kind of person with an established character that is reflected in a consistent set of behaviors that fosters the flourishing of others, and particularly when combined as a team. It is to this end that leaders must keep their head in the boat and eschew all outside distractions.

Chapter Six

THE HEART OF A TEAM

George Pocock learned much about the hearts and souls of young men. He learned to see hope where a boy thought there was no hope, to see skill where skill was obscured by ego or by anxiety. He observed the fragility of confidence and the redemptive power of trust. He detected the strength of the gossamer threads of affection that sometimes grew between a pair of young men or among a boatload of them striving honestly to do their best. And he came to understand how those almost mystical bonds of trust and affection, if nurtured correctly, might lift a crew above the ordinary sphere, transport it to a place where nine boys somehow became one thing.

— Daniel James Brown

Every team has an evolving emotional core. If the team is to achieve greatness, it begins with achieving emotional swing as well as technical swing. This is not possible without a leader who exhibits emotional intelligence. Herein lies the potential heart of the team. This is perhaps the most overlooked aspect of a leader's development and yet it is essential when leadership is applied to a team. It is not a new concept but has been buried of late by the 20th century's fixation on scientific data and rationalism at any cost.

In rowing, coaches can become fixated on 2K erg times and bench press and leg lift numbers. In rowing, everything is prone to quantification. This engineering attention to detail, while valuable, is not enough for a high-performance team. Here the relational intangibles matter—the emotional connections, the mutual affection, the irrevocable trust in one another—loom to the forefront of performance considerations. For it is under conditions of extreme personal pain, physical exhaustion, and intense competition where margins of victory are measured in hundredths of a second that these factors make the decisive difference.

The idea of emotional intelligence or "EQ" first appeared in Daniel Goleman's 1995 book, Emotional Intelligence: Why EQ Can Matter More than IQ. Since then, extensive research has been done on the concept both comparing emotional intelligence to intellectual intelligence as well as assessing its benefits to actual teams, organizations, and companies.

What many had intuited by anecdotal experience was confirmed. IQ and the other reductive measures of school achievement do not predict success in life or leadership. In fact, when compared side by side, high IQ predicts on average 6 percent of success whereas EQ is directly responsible for between 27 and 45 percent of job success. Overall effective leadership demands proficiency in three things: technical skills, cognitive abilities, and emotional intelligence. Of these three categories, emotional intelligence proved to be twice as important as the others for performance success. In senior leadership, the difference between a star performer and an average performer was ninety percent attributable to emotional intelligence. Effective team performance is dependent upon the application of emotional intelligence. It's the heart of a team.

What are the building blocks of emotional intelligence? According to Steven Stein and Howard Book in *The EQ Edge: Emotional Intelligence and Your Success*, "Emotional intelligence is made up of short-term, tactical, dynamic skills which can be brought into play as the situation warrants and can be improved by means of training, coaching, and experience." There are several models of emotional intelligence. The model here is based on Multi-Health Systems, Inc. It includes an assessment of five realms or building blocks of emotional and social functioning:
   1. Self-Perception
   2. Self-Expression
   3. Interpersonal
   4. Decision Making, and
   5. Stress Management.

Self-Perception
Self-perceptions realm includes the leaders' ability to know and manage themselves. Such self-awareness means having a deep understanding of one's emotions, strengths, weaknesses, needs, and drives. The goal here is to have an honest and realistic assessment of oneself—one that is neither too critical nor too confident.

Self-Expression
Self-expression deals with the way a leader faces the world. It balances one's assertiveness and independence with one's vulnerability and openness. Such a balance enhances whether people perceive you as authentic and approachable.

Interpersonal

The interpersonal realm includes the leaders' people skills—how they interact and get along with others. This realm has three parts:

1. Ability to make and maintain relationships
2. Degree of empathy towards others, and
3. Ability to exercise social responsibility to society at large.

Since leadership is grounded in followership and the mutual sharing of inspiration and trust, influence and purpose, the importance of interpersonal relationship skills is self-evident. Your ability and tendency to give and receive trust and compassion and to establish and maintain mutually satisfying personal relationships is pivotal to leadership success.

Decision Making

The decision-making realm involves the leaders' ability to use emotions in the best way to solve problems. Notice that this skill is not simply about solving problems, but the ability to solve problems in a manner that takes the emotional context of others into consideration. This realm also has three parts:

1. Impulse control
2. Reality testing, and
3. Problem-solving.

It is most often in the decision-making process that the leaders' commitment to returning authority, embracing ambiguity, and maintaining empathy when there are differences of opinion or overt conflict are most revealed.

Stress Management

Stress management has to do with being flexible, tolerant, and able to control your impulses. Under the conditions of crew racing, the ability to maintain focus and equanimity under pressure is an obvious advantage. The ability to maintain a realistically positive attitude in the face of adversity is a major strength.

The composite attitude when these other variables are addressed is happiness, a general satisfaction with life. When people have this, they bring a zest for living into the workplace or team.

Integrating EQ into the Whole

Emotional intelligence is not the same thing as personality. Like IQ personality is fixed and static. This enables personality tests to divide people into types. In contrast, emotional intelligence is always found on an evolving continuum involving strengths and weaknesses. But most importantly, emotional intelligence allows for the possibility for growth and change, particularly through training, coaching, and life experience.

An additional factor that should be considered when assessing one's strengths and weaknesses in emotional intelligence is that each category can be in isolation taken to an extreme. Too much self-regard can be viewed as arrogance or conceitedness. Too much self-actualization can lead to self-centeredness. Too much emotional self-awareness can cause hypersensitivity, and so on. Each of these factors needs to be assessed, present, and balanced with each other. In each team member, there needs to be emotional harmony as well as technical competence.

This balancing act cannot be done alone because of one's individual biases, which lead to behavioral blind spots. Such balance is only achieved in community and with the accountability of a trusted mentor. Moreover, because new emotional habits and behaviors need to be developed, this mentoring and accountability needs to be carried out over time within real life experiences. Put simply, emotional intelligence is not something that can be learned alone or from a book.

Nor can it be developed by good intentions alone. A stronger motivator than will is attachment. Because attachment is relational, attachment grows in the context of our connections to other people. Minimally, the leader's attachment to his or her mentor is critical. But even more decisive is the leaders' attachment to the other team members. When an individual has attachment love with others on his or her team, it forges in the individual an identity. Here the individual identity merges with the team identity, which forms the strongest and mutually reinforcing linkage between the leader and the other team members. The individual identity and the group identity experience a synchronicity of emotional alignment or emotional swing. In the end, we become who we love and who we love serves as the strongest motivator of changed behavior. At this level, swing is rooted in and animated by love. The deepest force that creates human character is relational and can only be forged through and in the experience of teamwork. Most ex-oarsmen will tell you that they learned more fundamentally important lessons about life in the racing shell than in the classroom. This is the relational forge—we must assume real life conflicts and disagreements—where character is developed, and emotional intelligence learned.

Linking Virtue to EQ Behaviors

There is a tendency to think of EQ in terms of amorphous feelings instead of concrete behaviors. This is a mistake and makes it impossible to evaluate progress and make constructive relational change. This can be overcome by overlapping the leadership virtues—love, integrity, truth, excellence, and relationships (LITER)—and the behavioral components of the EQ-i$^{2.0}$ model. This analysis was conducted by Hile Rutledge, president of Otto Kroeger Associates, a leading U.S. training center for EQ-i$^{2.0}$. When five virtues are compared to the fifteen aspirational behaviors of EQ, the following nine leadership priorities emerge:

Interpersonal

- Interpersonal relationships
- Empathy
- Social responsibility

Self-Expression

- Assertiveness
- Independence
- Problem solving

The Big Three

- Self-regard
- Self-actualization
- Optimism

It becomes important that leaders in partnership with their mentors work on the behaviors that need strengthening based on their EQ assessment and lived experience with others. In the end, EQ is not about feelings, but concrete relational behaviors. These can be changed.

Leadership Model

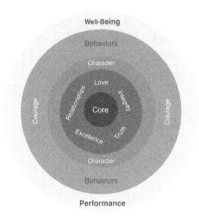

EQ-i Behaviors

Self-Regard	Interpersonal	Assertiveness
Self-Actualization	Relationships Empathy	Independence
Optimism	Social Responsibility	Problem Solving

What does it take to be a good team player? Emotional intelligence is at the heart of every successful team. For it is only with self-awareness, balance, and synchronicity that a team can meaningfully amp up the pain threshold to serve an attachment bond that transcends individual intention or motivation.

This is the core dynamic of every effective team though it is frequently overlooked. When Bobby Moch looked into the eyes of Don Hume at the close of the 1936 Olympic Gold medal race, and yelled, "Pick'er up! Pick'er up!" this is the unconscious neurological dynamic that kicked in, an affection animated emotional swing born of an aligned emotional intelligence between coxswain and stroke.

Stein and Book conclude, "It seems likely that emotionally intelligent players are more likely to have the staying power that leads to success as an athlete. This is something that professional coaches, scouts, and trainers in all areas of sport should take note of." Another word for the swing that this experience creates is joy, an overwhelming satisfaction with the process of living—to be able to embrace all aspects of life with cheerfulness and enthusiasm. Such teams have a magnetic attractiveness to others because belonging to something larger than oneself while being affirmed in one's own individual contribution is what we long for.

Coach Al Ulbrickson put his finger on the success of the 1936 U.S. Olympic team, "Every man in the boat had absolute confidence in every one of his mates.... Why they won cannot be attributed to individuals, not even the stroke of Don Hume. Heartfelt cooperation all spring was responsible for the victory." It is the mystical relational experience that only teamwork under pressure can meaningfully provide. Emotional intelligence is the leadership core of effective teams.

Chapter Seven

THE PARADOX
OF LEADERSHIP

Joe Rantz's mother died of throat cancer when he was five. Two years later, his father married a woman seventeen years his junior. Three children later, Joe's stepmother Thula became alienated from Joe. Daniel Brown writes, *"So began Joe's life in exile. Thula would no longer cook for him, so every morning before school and again every evening he trudged down the wagon road to the cookhouse at the bottom of the mountain to work for the company cook, Mother Cleveland, in exchange for breakfast and dinner.... He fed himself and made his way, but his world had grown dark, narrow, and lonely. There were no boys his age whom he could befriend in the camp."*

Connection fueled by emotional intelligence is much easier to achieve in theory on paper. It is much more difficult in real life. We all come to our work or to our teams with our life experiences and woundedness. Such was certainly the case of Joe Rantz. Connection for him was a foreign concept and a distant reality.

The same can be said of many leaders. Initially, leaders who pride themselves on their technical knowledge find their work world juxtaposed to their home life where connection is self-evidently needed. But soon leaders realize that relational connection is just as essential to their work world as well, particularly in building effective teams. This is because connection is the essence of the human experience.

Connection demands closer inspection. What fosters the potential for human connection? This question is explored by Joseph Luft and Harry Ingham in a four-paned window, which divides personal awareness into four different types, as represented by its four quadrants: Open, Hidden, Blind, and Unknown.

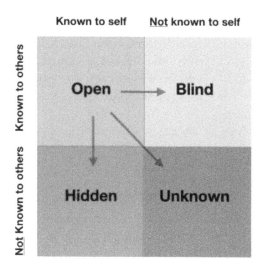

The Open quadrant represents things that both you know about yourself, and that people know about you. For example, you know your name and so do your colleagues and friends. Most will know some of your interests and family information. The knowledge represented here can include not only information but feelings, motives, behaviors, wants, needs, and desires... indeed, any information describing who you are. When you first meet a new person, the information held in this quadrant is not very large since there has been little time to exchange information.

In teams and working groups, a goal should be the development and expansion of the open area for every person, because when this area is expanded, people are more effective and productive. The open quadrant minimizes distortions and mistrust by providing opportunities for dialog on topics that are acknowledged as important.

The key to an effective open quadrant is the opportunity and willingness for self-disclosure. The challenge here is compounded when the team is functioning in a networked or virtual environment and this challenge should be consciously addressed.

The Hidden quadrant is where we keep the personal information that we do not want others to have access. The reasons for keeping information hidden can range from being sensitive information, that one would not want to share, to information that an employee would like to share, but does not feel there is adequate trust or safety to do so. In either of these situations, exposing information to the team can have negative repercussions. However, if the organization is based on trust and respect, then sharing relevant hidden information helps both the individual and the team.

Creating a safe emotional environment where this hidden information is safe to be shared is an essential barrier to creating an effective team. Connection requires creating a sense of belonging. What prevents connection is shame. To transcend shame involves vulnerability or allowing oneself to be known. The work of Brené Brown is salient.

Her TED Talk, "The Power of Vulnerability" is now one of the top five TED Talks of all time. The importance of embracing vulnerability for effective teams is why she has been brought in to counsel organizations as diverse as Microsoft, Pixar, and the Department of Defense. Creating a safe place for vulnerability, to shift the Hidden to Open, does not happen without leaders role modeling vulnerability and teams making this a priority. Brené Brown adds, "Vulnerability sounds like truth and feels like courage. Truth and courage aren't always comfortable, but they're never weakness." Nothing creates a stronger sense of belonging, loyalty, and group cohesion more than when a vulnerability is embraced.

Likewise, the Blind quadrant too holds the key to creating effective teams. This area involves information and behavior to which one is personally blind or unaware. When strengths and areas for development are shared in this quadrant, the recipient is better able to decide on embracing changes that better serve the team. The blind spots identified in this area can range from technical competence to attitudinal issues. Regardless of the feedback shared here, it needs to be data that helps the recipient become a better team member. This information expands the open area. A person can feel like they are being singled out or ganged up on unless feedback is a routine and regular part of a teams' dynamic. The Blue Angels, the flight demonstration squadron of the U.S. Navy, does a debrief and personal feedback session after every flight. In this case, regular feedback perfects performance and saves lives.

Ironically, it is the Unknown quadrant where the greatest potential for relational connection lies. The Unknown quadrant represents things that neither you nor others know about you. This quadrant taps into the fact that 95 percent of what motivates our behaviors stems from our unconscious mind. There is more that we don't know about ourselves—even when we are self-reflective—than we know. People are complex and there is much that is under the surface of the conscious mind. Shared living and events can surface feelings, thoughts, or interests that were never recognized before. These are instances where the Unknown area reveals clues to an inner life that has gone unnoticed. Recognizing these clues is important. They emerge over time through the experience of shared living.

To summarize, 1) self-disclosure reduces the Hidden area, 2) embracing vulnerability and creating a safe place reduces the Hidden area, 3) regular feedback reduces the Blind area, and 4) collectively in the process of living together they reduce the Unknown area. This is how connection is created both in the home and work environment where they are equally essential to the creation of an effective team.

"Joe was a good and popular student. His classmates found him outgoing, freewheeling, handy with a joke, and fun to be around. A few who got to know him better found that he could suddenly and unexpectedly turn somber—never nasty or hostile, but guarded, as if there was a part of him he didn't want you to touch."

We all come to the necessity of connection from our own lives and the wounds experienced therein. This was the reality of Joe Rantz. His mother had died when he was five. He had moved repeatedly during childhood. At fifteen he was abandoned by his family and learned to stoically survive alone. With steeled will and impressive resilience, he was selected to the first boat at the University of Washington rowing team. While the other boys headed to the shower, those selected to the first boat marched down to the lake for a celebratory row.

Daniel Brown continues,

> At the north end of the lake, the coxswain called out, "Way... 'nuff!" The boys stopped rowing and the shell glided to a stop, the long oars trailing in the water alongside them. Dark clouds fringed with silver moonlight scudded by overhead, carried briskly along by the winds aloft. The boys sat without talking, breathing heavily, exhaling flumes of white breath. Even now that they had stopped rowing, their breathing was synchronized, and for a brief, fragile moment it seemed to Joe as if all of them were part of a single thing, something alive with breath and spirit of its own.... Joe gulped huge drafts of the frigid air and sat staring at the scene, watching it turn into a soft of colors as, for the first time since his family had left him, tears filled his eyes.
>
> He turned his face to the water, fiddling with his oarlock so the others would not see. He didn't know where the tears had come from, what they were about. But something inside him had shifted, if only for a few moments.

It was a connection that moved him. He was now a part of a team, a new family, a living breathing thing larger than himself. The paradox of leadership is that it is not about the leader. Even more, a leader cannot truly become an effective leader without the investment of others in his or her life. For without others, genuine connection is not possible. It is in the connection that true leadership is found.

Chapter Eight

THE PRICE OF LEVELING UP

Crew races are not won by clones. They are won by crews, and great crews are carefully balanced blends of both physical abilities and personality types.... If they are going to row well together, each of these oarsmen must adjust to the needs and capabilities of the other. Each must be prepared to compromise something in the way of optimizing his stroke for the overall benefit of the boat.... Only in this way can the capabilities that come with diversity be turned to advantage rather than disadvantage.

— Daniel James Brown

When the University of Washington coach Al Ulbrickson invited the legendary boatbuilder George Pocock into the coach's launch, the boys in the boat knew that some changes to the lineup were inevitable. Ulbrickson was getting counsel from his resident-wise sage.

Balancing diversity in an organization as in a rowing shell requires listening, communication, and feedback. It demands an ongoing relational dynamic. This is not a book about leadership *per se*, but leadership in service to a team. Likewise, this is not a book about rowing, but a book about rowing an eight-person shell, which, including the coxswain and coach minimally, involves ten people. Put simply, the dynamics of team leadership cannot be learned in a single shell, only in a rowing eight. A team leader can only be formed in the presence of and with the involvement of other people. It is not something that can be learned from a book or accomplished as a solitary person. The making of a team leader is a collaborative task.

Having examined the attitudes needed to become a leader and the attributes required of leaders, we turn now to the process of becoming a leader, a process, which requires sustained accountability. This is how this balance is achieved.

Americans are unhappy at work: tension, boredom, and apathy prevail. The Gallup poll indicates that 49 percent of the workforce is not engaged, and 14 percent are totally disengaged. Taken together this means that at any one time roughly two-thirds of the team are not consciously involved in fulfilling the team's mission. In a rowing eight, if six of the oarsmen are not engaged, it is unlikely that the crew will leave the starting line much less finish a race. And yet, this kind of reality and performance is routinely accepted in most organizations and places of business. This is the norm, not the exception.

This tension is heightened among younger workers such as millennials who have an even higher set of expectations about their work experience. They want their work to have meaning and purpose. They want to use their talents and strengths to do what they do best every day. They want to learn and develop. They want their job to fit their life or more accurately to blend more fully with their identity. Instead, they find dysfunctional organizations blended with toxic leaders.

An organization is healthy when its culture, purpose, strategy, leadership, and followership fit together in an inclusive consistent way. Are people engaged or merely putting in their time? Do people trust each other? Is there a collective sense of purpose and enduring standards of excellence? Do people feel they are valued and are making a difference?

Such an organizational dynamic does not happen by accident. Nor does it happen automatically. It necessitates input from a leader. The leader sets the tone for her team.

On one hand, the authentic leader inspires, encourages, and develops each member of the team and, in so doing, betters the team. Team members know their backs are covered. They have support and will not be hung out to dry if something does not go as planned. Every person counts and is counted on.

On the other hand, the leader can also be toxic. The team's purpose or mission is vague. Roles and responsibilities are not clearly defined. There is little communication in the form of helpful feedback. Micromanagement is often the order of the day. Results are less than expected and one's work is reduced to merely a job. People deserve a leader who inspires, who leads by example; not one who extinguishes the life and potential of the team.

A healthy organization or team is one that displays:
- Clarity of purpose
- An engaged workforce
- High morale
- High retention rates

- Clear communication
- Constructive feedback, and
- Openness to learning.

A healthy organization breeds high performance, defined as the ability to deliver meaningful, measurable, and financially sustainable results for the people and causes the organization is in existence to serve.

The leader within the organization must create a structural roundtable. Going back to our Roundtable metaphor, most organizations are only comprised of a king and an assortment of noble knights. Critically missing are Merlin and Dagonet—the wise sage and the court jester. Most organizations surround their leaders with yes men: men who are unwilling or fearful of providing feedback. College president Steven B. Sample—the man who turned the University of Southern California into one of the most respected and highly rated universities in the country—did so by advocating for contrarian leadership, an organizational structure that championed contrarian perspectives. This is what Merlin provides, namely the wisdom of history and age. This is what Dagonet provides, namely personal self-criticism that given with humor reveals the king's blind spots. Unless these roles are structured within the culture of an organization, trust and inspiration, the key to the leadership/followership dynamic, will be forfeited. There is wisdom to be found in Camelot.

Two areas are particularly indicative of an effective roundtable or healthy organization: feedback and micromanaging.

Feedback

Constructive feedback involves discussions about performance, strengths and areas for growth. Project performance—where things went well and which areas need improving, including overall team performance—includes strengths and areas that need further attention. This feedback needs to go in both directions from the team to the leader and from the leader to the team.

Holding your cards closely and not saying what needs to be said undermines an effective team. Open communication has two additional aspects. First, it helps to improve overall performance. Issues are identified and resolved early before they become problems. When individual and team performance is reviewed, people have an opportunity to reflect on their work, make changes and revise plans that ultimately result in improved results and greater personal satisfaction.

Second, open communication creates opportunities for honest and frank dialog. It is important for the discussions to be specific, not generalized so that the leader gets to know his people on a deeper level. How can we improve? What's lurking around the corner? When people feel they are in an environment where their input is valued and taken seriously, seeds of trust are planted, and extraordinary teams begin to bloom.

Rebecca Knight in her article, "How to Give Your Team Feedback," makes the following recommendations.

1. Set expectations early – It is less about being an approachable leader as having feedback routinely structured into every aspect of the organization.

2. Ask general questions – Create a safe environment where honesty and candor are rewarded.
3. Work your way up to structured reviews – Once a general expectation that everything is going to be subject to a debrief and a feedback review, you can then structure more formal reviews. Until the culture of feedback is established, the more formal structured reviews will not achieve the desired results.
4. Keep performance issues out in the open – The management mantra, "Praise in public, criticize in private" does not serve well in team settings. When teams have problems, feedback should all be out in the open.
5. Foster team relationships – Conflict within a team is inevitable, encourage the team to resolve these conflicts themselves.
6. Debrief every project – Something can be learned about performance after every team effort, so encourage the team to realize that they are being reviewed not simply as individuals but as a team.

Summary Principles

Do:
- Make sure the team understands that feedback is a shared leadership responsibility; it is less the responsibility of Arthur as the knights.
- Schedule routine check-in meetings.
- Keep the tone positive by encouraging team members to say what they appreciate about others' contributions.

Don't:
- Start the meeting with your own feedback for the team, return authority to the team.
- Shy away from performance issues, address them openly as a group.
- Get in the middle of personality conflicts, rather than facilitate difficult conversations.

Keep **S-B-I-I*** in mind when giving or receiving feedback:

S – **Situation**: describe the specific time and place.

B – **Behavior**: what did you observe—make it factual.

I – **Impact**: what consequences did you hear/see—make it factual.

I – **Intent**: ask what the person's intent was behind the behavior—to provide insight on why they acted the way they did.

* (Center for Creative Leadership)

And finally, the relational dynamic being encouraged here is not about friendship as much as team performance. The best way to build relationships with your employees is to improve how you work together, not to take a break from working through social activities.

Micromanagement
The second area that directly affects the organizational climate or team dynamic is the use of micromanagement. Here are some signs of a classic micromanager:

- You're never quite satisfied with deliverables.
- You often feel frustrated because you would've gone about the task differently.
- You laser in on the details and take great pride and pain in making corrections.
- You constantly want to know where all your team members are and what they're working on.
- You ask for frequent updates on where things stand.
- You prefer to be cc'd on all emails.

For many, this is a delicate subject as many have been subject to this kind of management style. One can acknowledge that there are times when careful close monitoring and careful follow-up is needed such as in an extreme crisis. But in general micromanagement does not serve well as a long-term leadership style. It breeds distrust and creates a barrier to meaningful communication and feedback. It is either a sign of the leader's insecurity or lack of leadership development. The results of micromanagement are a decrease in team cohesion and general apathy.

Executive coach Muriel Wilkins provides four suggestions if you want to stop micromanaging.

1. Get over yourself. There are always rationalizations for this kind of behavior, but the negative consequences are generally far greater than these reasons.
2. Let it go. The difference in management and micromanagement is in the level of detail. Avoid the minutia.
3. Give the "what," not the "how." There is nothing wrong with high expectations about

deliverables. The difference is dictating how to get that result. Articulate the vision, not the means of getting there.

4. Expect to win. The underlying psychological factor revealed in micromanaging is a fear of failure. Unresolved, this fear can lead to failure. Empower your team and expect excellent results.

Team leadership demands effective two-way communication. Encouraging feedback and minimizing micromanaging are essential to fostering a good organizational climate. Feedback is a catalyst for healthy teams, while micromanagement produces a toxic and dysfunctional atmosphere for team performance.

Marketing guru Seth Godin observes that when people submit a short bio and are given the opportunity to update their bios after seeing the others' bios in their class, the bios always get better. He concludes, "It's not because people didn't try the first time. It's because being surrounded by people on the same journey as you, causes you to level up. Your path forward is pretty simple: Decide on your journey and find some people who will cause you to level up."

The diversity of an effective team needs to be balanced by constructive feedback and trusting delegation. A team requires a certain kind of leader, and a leader requires a certain kind of team. Both need each other for mutual leveling up. In this environment where open honest communication is celebrated and high standards expected, teams as teams rather than as mere individuals can achieve more than the sum of its individual parts.

Chapter Nine

COMPONENTS OF HIGH PERFORMANCE

Where is the spiritual value of rowing? The losing of self entirely to the cooperative effort of the crew as a whole.

— George Pocock

Organizations are complex. Dysfunction within organizations is common. Typically, these dysfunctions are approached as individual problems to be solved: a lack of skilled labor, high employee turnover, a disengaged workforce, unethical behavior, and so on. You cannot solve the problems of an organization by focusing on an individual component. Instead, one must take a holistic systems-based perspective on organizational performance. To improve the wine, do not focus on the grape, focus on the terroir. Terroir is a French term used in winemaking to describe the complete natural environment in which a particular wine is produced, including factors such as the soil, topography, and climate. For it is in the interactive dynamics or ecosystem between the various parts that creates a distinctive wine or the high performance in a team. Swing is an interactive dynamic of key organizational elements and not the perfection of one single thing.

There are three key elements to swing, which must be synchronized into a harmonious whole in real time under the extreme pressure of competition—a ballet of pain as rowing is often described and experienced. We have spoken of the preparatory attitudes needed for swing and the attributes necessary for it to emerge. It is now time to discuss the key elements that must be harmonized in practice. How does one pull it all together? How does one make poetry out of the various parts? Swing is elusive, but it's not impossible to achieve for any crew. In the end, swing is not about winning, but rather achieving the maximum potential from a team with consistency when under stress. It is about achieving a collective harmony forged through the mental and physical breaking point of each individual sacrificed to this collective harmony.

The three elements that must be harmonized for swing are leadership (both inside the shell represented by the coxswain and outside the shell represented by the coach), technical competence, and organizational expertise. Let's look at each element more closely.

Leadership is paramount to achieving organizational excellence. A leader's character, behavior, humility, selfless courage, and commitment to serve others above self must be resolute. Leadership makes or breaks an organization. The leader is the "cork in the bottle" when it comes to organizational performance—either blocking its potential or letting it flow. The decision to embrace those qualities that release this resourcefulness of the team always starts from the leader. An organization can succeed because of a leader, but not despite a leader. This is because a leader embodies technical competence and organizational expertise and at the same time empowers the same within the organization. The natural entropy of an organization if left on its own is toward fragmentation and failure. Swing and harmonized performance always require the successful example and input of leaders. Put simply, leadership is necessary but not sufficient to achieve swing.

The second key element of organizational performance is technical competence. It is having the appropriate level of knowledge, technical proficiency, skill, experience and training for one's profession or given team assignment. This element is given the most attention within an organization and is perhaps the easiest to identify and fix. A teacher must have subject matter mastery and the ability to connect with his or her students. Of the two components of a great teacher, mastery is much easier to achieve than connection. The adage attributed to Theodore Roosevelt, "They don't care how much you know until they know how much you care," bears this out in classroom after classroom. This points to the third element.

The third key element is organizational expertise. It is having both an understanding of organizational dynamics as well as the behaviors associated with emotional intelligence to release and encourage the best from the organization's people. Attitudes and behaviors associated with this element include:
- Focusing on building a team
- Understanding that behavior speaks louder than words
- Establishing standards of excellence and holding people accountable to these standards
- Clearly communicating and reinforcing purpose and mission

- Developing the organization's identity and distinctiveness
- Establishing healthy relationships throughout the organization
- Building the capacity of skills and abilities of every person
- Encouraging collaborative teamwork
- Listening before acting when and where needed
- Creating an environment where receiving and giving constructive feedback and expressing appreciation is a routine part of the organizational life.

When a leader can inspire people and mold them into a team, they develop trust. When this occurs, they have a set of conditions for further development and success. Trust engenders confidence, commitment, and a *esprit de corps* that is unbeatable.

Leadership, Technical Competence, and Organizational Expertise are the three key elements of organizational performance. More important than knowing what they are, is knowing how they interact within an organization. There are four possible interactions between a leader's technical competence (TC) and organizational expertise (OE).

The Leader

	Capability but at a cost	E* Capability for sustained *Excellence*
Technical Competence		
	Failure	Limited Capability

Organizational
Expertise

Failure (low TC / low OE)

The leader does not have the core competency to set the vision, tone, and ethos for the organization. The organization does not have the trust, behaviors, or capabilities to succeed. Without conscious and continual input from leaders, the natural entropy of an organization will always move in this direction.

Limited Capacity to Succeed (low TC / high OE)

Having a high level of organizational expertise cannot overcome a lack of technical competence in a leader or the organization. If the leader has low TC, he will have a troublesome time building trust and confidence with his followers. If the organization is low in TC, performance will suffer until the leader can identify and fill the gaps with proper training to raise TC.

A high level of organizational expertise can help in the development of people and their technical competence, depending on how quickly the problem is addressed. However, often it is "too little, too late" to be successful. Since organizations don't normally have the luxury of taking time off for training, the training has to take place while the plane is in the air, frequently the organization finds itself too far behind the developmental curve. Sometimes management will put a new leadership team in place to address the problems but not give them the time or space to address them. This sets up the new leadership for failure.

Capability But at a Cost (high TC / low OE)
This organization's performance is often the most difficult to diagnose. It is viewed as good, perhaps even excellent on paper, but has uneven results. When technical competence is high and organizational expertise is low, leadership tends to "drive" the organization through micr0management and centralized control with little regard or appreciation for their people. All too often people in this situation are viewed as secondary to the mission. The mantra reverberates, "Get the job done, whatever the cost." This is sometimes referred to as a "mercenary organization."

This is where it becomes costly: the visible technical competence masks the invisible relational connectivity. People are shredded. They become discouraged, disengaged, and do only what is necessary. Constructive feedback between the leader and his team is rare and lost are opportunities for a team to highlight potential problems, offer alternative solutions or suggest needed improvements. Because the problems are often more personal and subjective, they proceed without being addressed. The results:

- Fluctuating performance
- Minimal organizational resiliency
- Lack of trust

- Costly and inefficient work and programs
- Leader's lack of compassion engraved into the fabric of the organization
- Low morale and retention rates, work is no longer fun, and
- Loss of talented people.

Leadership is about people. When leaders ignore this, they ignore it at their own risk, as well as at the risk to their people and mission.

E* or Sustained Excellence (high TC / high OE)
This organization has the capability for sustained excellence across the board. Though their performance will have normal fluctuations, they can right themselves and learn from their experiences. They have resilience in both times of success and failure. No crew is going to win every race. The story of the 1936 crew team gold medalist was a three-year journey. Even when the team became very good, and won the West Coast championships, they lost in the national finals. It was only after this loss and maybe because of it, did they rebound to win the Olympic gold medal.

The leader of an E* team has developed solid technical competence and organizational expertise within herself, as well as those within her organization. She is authentic, knows her strengths and weaknesses, and recognizes that "excellence" begins with her own behavior and actions.

There are high levels of trust throughout the organization. Everyone knows their role and responsibilities. They feel accountable for their actions, responsible to each other, and are focused on mission success, organizational improvement, and personal growth. The team is fully engaged.

People want to make a difference. People want to be fully engaged in their work. People long to experience an E* team. They want leaders of character who strive for excellence, who desire to serve and inspire and show the way. The winning edge every winning shell has over its competition is the same for every winning organization— the people in the boat. George Pocock made this point long ago, "There are no fast boats: only fast crews." It is always the people who make the difference.

Excellence is not a synonym for perfection or success. Rather excellence is:
- An innate and unrelenting passion within a person or an organization to continually
  - Pursue continual improvement, always building upon yesterday's achievements
  - Build personal relationships and organizational mastery
  - Admit and learn from mistakes
  - Seek better practices and processes
  - Develop integrated and cohesive teamwork and support
  - Setting high standards, holding people accountable to these standards
  - Not being satisfied with today's performance or results
  - Learn from both success and failure
- About the sustained pursuit of a worthy goal, a mission, a purpose
- A lifelong journey of learning and growing.

Excellence is about more than just winning a particular race.

The journey of excellence leads to sustained, exemplary levels of performance. Organizations with a sustained pursuit of excellence have an engaged and highly motivated workforce, high levels of trust, well integrated teams, better outcomes, and better bottom line economically, socially, environmentally, and spiritually.

Make no mistake about it, the development of an E^* organization is extremely challenging and often messy work. It takes time and dedication. Yet this is the task and responsibility of every leader. An E^* organization is about achieving sustained excellence and experiencing the satisfaction that you have made the difference. Pocock summarizes, "When you get the rhythm in an eight, it's pure pleasure to be in it. It's easy work when the rhythm comes—that "swing" as they call it. I've heard men shriek out with delight when the swing came in an eight; it's a thing they'll never forget as long as they live."

Chapter Ten

EMOTIONAL INTELLIGENCE IN PRACTICE

When the best leader's work is done, the people say, 'We did it ourselves.'

— Lao Tzu

We tend to limit discussions of leadership to the leader. More appropriately they should be focused on the team or organization. When we talk about emotional intelligence [EQ], too often our thinking is limited to the psychological characteristics of an individual. In fact, where they have the most impact is when they become the general ethos of the team. A premise of team leadership is that the public face of the leader is eventually subsumed by the self-leadership of the team. Here the mission, virtues, self-governance, and EQ behavior are owned by the collective.

John A. Byrne is the founder and editor-in-chief of C-Change Media. He writes, "Success will belong to companies that are leaderless—or to be more precise, companies whose leadership is so widely shared that they resemble beehives, ant colonies, or schools of fish." Here the face of the organization is the organization itself. The leader holds them accountable to the process and results, without necessarily asserting himself into the action.

There is an irony here in that great teams need both an external leader for accountability as well as an internal leader. They instill the dynamic and discipline that keeps the group from the entropy of fragmentation. And yet when success is achieved, the best teams say, "We did it ourselves."

The effective work of a leader is catalytic. He increases the rate of a reaction without himself being changed. Effective teams need leadership, but only the kind of catalytic leader who returns authority to the group and empowers them to take ownership of the organization's mission, virtues, and emotional intelligence, and holds them accountable to both the process and results. An organization that calls significant attention to the leader is not an organization that is simultaneously calling attention to the importance of the team as a team. Listen to how a winning quarterback talks about the game in the post-game press conference.

Emotional intelligence came into the world as a body of research focusing on the behaviors that people engage in and the impact that these behaviors have on individual roles and interactions—even our well-being. Emotional intelligence is about and from human behavior and most importantly manifests itself within the group. Ideally, it has a systemic impact. EQ in a leader is a means of fostering EQ in the team.

There are many models and tools in the field of Emotional Intelligence. The most popular and referenced of these is the EQ-i$^{2.0}$ published by Multi-Health Systems (MHS) out of Toronto, Canada. The EQ-i model of Emotional Intelligence is comprised of fifteen core behaviors that can be understood, engaged, and even measured on both the individual and group levels. A leader can be Assertive, but so can an organization. An individual can be Optimistic, but so can a team. What follows are summaries of each of these fifteen behaviors and what each looks and sounds like (when developed and when overlooked) in teams and organizations.

Every NFL team has a bye week in their seventeen-game season. This is the one week without a game. It allows for team members to heal and for special plays to be practiced without the pressure of facing a new team in a week or less. How teams and team members use the bye week is a good indicator of how they rank on their collective EQ profile.

Self-Regard: Confidence in the Team
Self-regard is the ability and the tendency for a team with full recognition of its strengths and weaknesses to both like and have confidence in the team. Self-regard is frequently a concept used to describe NFL teams when it becomes apparent that collectively they believe in their ability to win games and overcome obstacles together. Perhaps this is most apparent when the persons personal life and public life blend together—when one's individual identity is framed increasingly as a team identity. Wearing the team colors is a personal fashion statement. What is interesting to note here is that personal concerns are valued and not discounted. It is only in this manner that the individuals' dreams can merge with that of the team.

Organizations that value self-regard
- Act with pride and self-confidence
- "I" statements about accomplishments abound

- Achievements are noticed, discussed, praised, and on display
- Evidence of people's personal lives and passions are on display

Organizations that overlook self-regard
- Mistake self-confidence and pride for arrogance
- "I" statements are discouraged
- People wanting acknowledgement is regarded as selfish or a sign of insecurity
- Personal issues are seen as distracting

Self-Actualization: Commitment to Growth
Self-actualization refers to a team's ability to grow and strive—to see potential, set meaningful goals, and work toward the betterment and fulfillment of the team. Not team ever arrives. But teams with high EQ collectively embrace the goal of becoming better and achieving the next goal together. Some have described this as a, "learning organization." What this describes is more than individual learning but rather everyone committing together for a shared goal of growth and improvement.

Organizations that value self-actualization
- Demonstrate ambition and drive toward goals
- Discuss progress, how to grow and advance, and what comes next
- Exert observable energy planning and pushing forward

Organizations that overlook self-actualization
- Treat the future and its challenges with complacency

- Exhibit comfort or resignation with life or work as it currently is
- Focus little time or effort on the future or growth

Emotional Self-Awareness: Permission to Feel

Emotional self-awareness relates to your ability and tendency to know what you are feeling and why. There are two challenges here. First is acknowledging these emotions, which is typically difficult for men and within some kinds of organizations. Second is being willing to explore why one is feeling these feelings. Activist organizations often do not prioritize the mindfulness and self-reflective space needed for such collective self-awareness. Others do not create the emotional safety that such vulnerability demands.

Organizations that value emotional self-awareness

- Recognize and acknowledge people for being aware of what they are feeling
- Take the time regularly to check-in on how people are feeling
- Emotional vocabulary of the group is rich, which is evidence of vulnerability
- People understand what triggers their emotions

Organizations that overlook emotional self-awareness

- Seem not to care if people know what they are feeling
- People tend not to talk about feelings, and when they do it's viewed as a weakness, joke, or secondary
- People don't connect the mood of the group with the events of the moment.

Emotional Expression: Permission to Emote

Emotional expression is related to emotional self-awareness above but is the degree to which there is a willingness to share, to be vulnerable, and be transparent with one's feelings. One is a measure of awareness, whereas this measures actual behaviors of emotional expression.

Organizations that value emotional expression

- Are often open, disclosing, and emotive
- Demonstrate an array of emotions, including both excitement and anger
- Leadership is easy to read as they demonstrate their emotions
- Organization values authenticity and transparency

Organizations that overlook emotional expression

- Tend to be cautious and reserved in their communication and engagement
- Demonstrate a steady, flat emotional tone with no observable difference between good times and bad
- Value control and caution even at the expense of authenticity.

Assertiveness: Acting on a Unified Identity

Assertiveness relates to your team's ability to put your needs, thoughts, and opinions out into the world, even when it might invite conflict. This reflects having a strong sense of self even in the face of opposition. Another way to look at this is that a strong sense of self reflects having a cohesive and united identity. An important, though an often-overlooked aspect of assertiveness, is a welcoming invitation to the contrarian voice. Many organizational roundtables lack the wise sage seen in the character of Merlin in King Arthur's Camelot who provides historical perspective and the court jester seen in the character of the knight Dagonet who provides an outside view that insider yes-men fail to provide. An emotionally healthy organization celebrates contrarian views in its ongoing commitment to improvement.

Organizations that value assertiveness
- Expect command and control behaviors and see them as useful
- Expect and encourage critique, appropriate opposition, and disagreement
- Rewards with praise, promotion, and power those people who speak up
- Value bold statements and critique as helpful, if not essential

Organizations that overlook assertiveness
- Discourage critique and debate
- Resist contrarian views
- Overlook or silence opposition, argument, and critique.

Independence: Can Go It Alone
Independence refers to the team's ability to be self-directed, to go it alone whenever needed. There is always pressure for individuals and organizations to follow the crowd, to avoid risk by following the status quo and the expected. A clear reflection of a team having a strong sense of cohesive identity is their ability to be innovative

with confidence. Teams will not get ahead simply by doing what everyone else is doing. Success demands thinking outside the box. Note that this characteristic puts necessary ongoing tension in collective action, a tension that is beneficial for strong teams and is generally only tolerated in them. Innovation requires time and space for reflection. Consequently, activist organizations are not going to be innovative because space for fresh thinking is not encouraged.

Organizations that value independence
- Seek, expect, evaluate, and reward individual effort
- Value being competent and right
- Notice, value, and emphasize innovative contributions
- Value and respect time spent alone.

Organizations that overlook independence
- Seem comfortable following the leader and/or believing the data offered by others
- Devalue or ignore new contributions and achievements of individuals
- Tend not to value or give time to and space for reflection
- Tend not to discuss, acknowledge, or celebrate individual achievements and contributions.

Interpersonal Relationships: Friendship with a Purpose
Interpersonal relationships related to a team's ability to give and receive trust and compassion. It is a measure of the organization establishing and maintaining mutually satisfying personal relationships. Organizations that place too much emphasis on missional solidarity will become

mercenary, using people rather than respecting them. Here, organizations must balance solidarity with relational sociality. This sociality is not simply about being friends or getting along but doing so in the context of getting results in moving the organization's mission forward. It is a relational emphasis that serves results. It is solidary to mission that gives one a sense of significance but sociality with one's team members that provides security. The combination of significance and security are psychologically necessary for high performance.

Organizations that value interpersonal relationships

- Offer and expect trust from one another
- Witness team members asking for help and support from others
- Maintain a warm and open environment so people care and share information

Organizations that overlook interpersonal relationships

- Promotes sharing and openness on a need-to-know basis
- Regard asking for help and giving compliments as unnecessary
- Do not regard trust as an important work necessity
- Smiling, friendly exchanges, and personal connections are infrequent.

Empathy: Awareness of Others
Empathy is the team's ability to take notice of, be sensitive to, and do something about other people's needs and feelings. Creating the conditions where needs and feelings are noticed is an obvious first barrier. But this is not enough. Action must be taken to address them concretely.

Listening needs to become a high value practice at all levels of the organization.

Organizations that value empathy
- Routinely ask for and consider people's needs and perspectives in meetings and discussions
- Witness people asking about and listening to other people's needs, opinions, and feelings
- Spend time in meetings and discussions hearing from and understanding everyone, particularly those who are inclined to be quiet

Organizations that overlook empathy
- Leadership makes decisions heedless of their impact on people
- Witness people on the team not speaking to or caring for other people's needs, opinions, and feelings
- Regard energy and time spent on sensitivity, caring, and curiosity of others as inefficient and a waste of resources.

Social Responsibility: Serve a Higher Cause

Social responsibility is the team's ability and tendency to cooperate and contribute to the welfare of a larger social system or organizational context and act with a consciousness that shows concern for and serves the greater common good. This trait is particularly important for younger workers who place a high value on their work making a meaningful difference in the world. This means that the organization must be committed to collective altruism that exceeds just winning or one's own bottom line.

Organizations that value social responsibility

- Are clearly serving something beyond self
- Emphasize and reward collective work
- Expect and respect sensitivity to others
- Respect "taking one for the team"

Organizations that overlook social responsibility

- Are not seen or regarded as client or customer-centric
- Lack a unifying compelling cause
- Have no direct connection to or concern for the wider community
- Struggle to get team members to think about and act for the greater good.

Problem Solving: Emotions as a Tool

Problem solving involves the team's ability and tendency to solve problems that involve emotions and to use emotions as an effective problem-solving tool. This is a results-oriented effort that works with, not despite, the team's emotions. It is, in effect, using empathy as a problem-solving strategy. Paramount here is one's attitude toward conflict and disagreement.

Organizations that value problem solving

- Witness people addressing disagreements and acknowledging feelings
- Foster open discussions about differing goals, ideas, and values
- Solves problems and engages conflict, seeing both as an opportunity for growth

Organizations that overlook problem solving

- Avoids conflict
- Discounts the emotional side of problems and disagreements, leaving them undiscussed
- Views disagreements and conflicts as a hindrance or roadblock to mission.

Reality Testing: Objective Metrics

Reality testing is the team's ability and tendency to assess honestly the here-and-now reality of any given moment or situation. What is really going on? There is always a strong pressure to describe a given moment or situation in terms of what we would like for it to be rather than what it is. One cannot get to "ought," without an honest assessment of what "is." This also requires prudential tension whereby narrower quantitative metrics must be balanced with broader qualitative metrics. In both cases, however, evidential metrics must have precedence over emotions. This variable deals primarily with how conflict is approached and resolved.

Organizations that value reality testing

- Have objective, fact-based conversations
- Take time to confirm perceptions and encourage objectivity
- Use words carefully
- Value and acknowledge people who change or moderate their moods when facts or understandings change

Organizations that overlook reality testing

- Evolve a volatile atmosphere
- Exhibit a level of drama where overstatement is common

- Engage in emotional reasoning—wherein people conclude that their feelings and emotional reactions prove something true, regardless of evidence.

Impulse Control: Constraint for the Team

Impulse control relates to the team's ability and willingness to delay taking an action or stating something that is inappropriate. It means that individual reactions are restrained by how they will impact the team. It eschews drama for the sake of drama. Critical here is the everyday use of humor and teasing, which can easily create the conditions whereby this boundary can be crossed. This can be in tension with assertiveness. It means that assertiveness is not an end but must be balanced by an ongoing consideration in what is best for the team. Here assertiveness is balanced by empathy to achieve impulse control.

Organizations that value impulse control
- Value a quiet, emotionally contained environment
- Seek and reward careful and thoughtful contributions
- Stress cautious and precise decision making

Organizations that overlook impulse control
- Do not value, recognize, or reward verbal caution and restraint
- May be or appear reactive.

Flexibility: Willingness to Adjust

Flexibility is the team's ability and tendency to adjust emotions, thoughts, and behavior to changing situations and conditions. In short, it is the ability to adapt, which demands being a learning growing team that can take in new data and change one's mind and approach. This suggests that a "by-the-book" approach is not always in the best interest of the team's high-level performance.

Organizations that value flexibility
- View their world and work as quickly changing that demand innovation for surivival
- Exhibits humility in terms of past approaches
- Exhibits openness to new data and approaches
- Encourages people to ask question with a spirit of exploration

Organizations that overlook flexibility
- See change as a threat
- Are rigid and arrogant
- Spend energy maintaining the status quo
- Resist change, preferring safety and efficiency to risk and innovation.

Stress Tolerance: Play the Long Game
Stress tolerance relates to the team's ability to work effectively under conditions of stress. This demands that the organization take the long view and manage work/life balance. It is not simply that one can gut it out in a sprint, but more importantly that one has resilience and sustainability for the long haul.

Organizations that value stress tolerance
- View their mission as requiring endurance
- Encourage the development of strong stress management skills

- Witness people engaging in self-care through such activities as exercise, rest, meditation, and work/life programs
- Engage in new challenges, even scary ones

Organizations that overlook stress tolerance
- Allow and foster stress, anxiety, and fear
- Avoid new challenges for fear of stress
- Do not regard stress management skills as a priority.

Optimism: Animating Hope

Optimism is the team's ability and tendency to look maintain a positive attitude even in the face of adversity. Optimism provides the team with hope and enables them to seek the future as positive. This is an important measure because it is the cumulative effect of the other variables. It is less an end as the inevitable fruit of the other variables combined in practice.

Organizations that value optimism
- Frequently express hope and a belief in the future and count on a positive outcome
- Regard bad times and setbacks as momentary disappointments, not predictors of what is to come
- Witness leadership looking to and speaking of the future as a place of growth, stability, and success both as an organization as well as for the team member

Organizations that overlook optimism
- Tend to regard the future as a place of stress, doubt, and disappointment

- Great statements of positivity with skepticism or doubt
- Use setbacks or disappointments as evidence to confirm the negative.

When these fifteen EQ components become a regular part of an organization's culture and routine behavior, we can speak of an EQ team:

1. Confidence in the Team
2. Commitment to Growth
3. Permission to Feel
4. Permission to Emote
5. Acting on a United Identity
6. Can Go It Alone
7. Friendships with a Purpose
8. Awareness of Others
9. Serve a Higher Cause
10. Emotions as a Tool
11. Objective Metrics
12. Constraint for the Team
13. Willingness to Adjust
14. Play the Long Game
15. Animating Hope

It becomes quite apparent that individual EQ is not all that is needed for an effective team. Rather these fifteen EQ characteristics need to be infused into the cultural expectations and routine behavior of the organization. Any honest team leader will recognize that this is a daunting task. Perfection is not what is needed in highly effective teams, rather an honest acknowledgement of what needs to be addressed and a consistent public plan to address them. A competent leader enlists input from the team as to their assessment of how the team is doing on each of the fifteen EQ components and prioritizes a plan together to address the most flagrant needs. Perfection is not found in the play but in the pilgrimage— a willingness to work together on becoming all that one can be in terms of a healthy EQ team.

Some of these EQ characteristics are more foundational than others. Some are the inevitable fruit or consequence of the existence of others. One must always start with the most foundational.

Finally, some of these EQ characteristics are designed to be in conscious tension with other characteristics. When this appears to be the case, it is best to redefine each characteristic in terms of the other. What is in view here is not a recipe with individual ingredients but rather a collective ecosystem of overlapping healthy emotional characteristics. It is the collective combination of them that ultimately makes the difference in performance. Remember it is the terroir not the grape that matters most in a winning wine. The goal is an EQ ethos across the entire team in every aspect of its collective life together.

Chapter Eleven

A FUSION OF INDIVIDUALS

Every man in the boat had absolute confidence in
every one of his mates.... Why they won cannot
be attributed to individuals, not even to the
stroke of Don Hume. Heartfelt cooperation all
spring was responsible for the victory.

— Al Ulbrickson

High-performance leadership begins with the attitude in
the leader that development is needed and possible and
then begins on this pilgrimage. The aim of this attitude is
to embody the attributes of transcendent virtues. This is
accomplished with the accountability of a mentor who
assesses the emotional intelligence of the leader and the
team and incrementally begins the process of establishing
trust, affection, and shared commitment to growth and
mutuality. The essence of leadership is this dynamic in the
leader-follower relationship. When a team is more than
one individual, it is the relational dynamic between the
leader and each team member as well as between each
team member that matters. Each person brings a unique
combination of experience, knowledge, skills, abilities,
and personality to the team. Fusing these into a seamless
whole is the task of the leader and the ultimate measure
of a team. High performance is the consequence, but not
the aim. The aim is this fusion. The individuals must be
first turned into a team.

The burden of this book is primarily to make the case that this process is essential, is often overlooked, and requires a different kind of leader than is usually celebrated. The ultimate measure of an elite high-performing team leader is his or her ability foster this fusion of individuals.

There is no one-size-fits-all recipe for this. Every individual is different. Every collection of individuals is different. Every situation that they face together is different. But what is always the same is that the relational dynamic between the leader and follower is paramount for success.

This demands that a leader be able to know her own strengths and weaknesses. Be able to assess the same in each team member and work incrementally toward a collective attunement of passion and purpose.

This will require that the leader actively return authority to the team, empower them in their technical skills and relational competence, and then get out of the way, effecting a kind of invisible enabling.

This is what we see in acted in the 1936 Olympic gold medal race. The coach's directive that Don Hume was too sick to race was challenged by the team. The coach listened to the team and got out of the way. In this way, they were collectively empowered to face the inevitable obstacles that the race brought to them. It was their race. The coach was not in the boat and could at that point have no direct influence on the results. But by creating the long-sustained dynamics between the oarsmen over the course of the previous months together, they were able to rally for a come from behind victory over two powerful state-sponsored crews from Germany and Italy.

The lasting point here is that there are two senses of swing. There is the technical swing in the rowing of the boat when perfect harmony is achieved in the fusion of each stroke. But even more important, and more difficult to achieve, is the fusion of the relational dynamics of trust and inspiration between the oarsmen. In the end, it is relational swing that must be the aim of all team leaders. Here the combined dynamics of trust, character, humility, and vulnerability are put to the test in the crucible of individual pain and collective competition. This is the "heartfelt cooperation" of which Al Ulbrickson spoke. This is the measure of elite leaders of high-performance teams. This is the highest form of swing.

Chapter Twelve

BEST VERSION OF SELF

Harmony, balance, rhythm, there you have it. That's what life is all about.

— George Pocock

Swing does not occur in a racing shell unless there is harmony, balance, and rhythm. For this to happen, there needs to be an outside observer who is willing to spend time observing, listening, challenging, and encouraging the oarsman, individually and as a team, moving them beyond themselves to something greater, from individual achievement to team greatness. While Ulbrickson developed the rowing tangibles of the team, Pocock worked on their intangibles—their hearts. Both were needed if they were ever to reach for the stars.

Our personal lives are no different. We will never experience swing until there is a deep internal sense of harmony, balance, and rhythm. It is not something we can will into place. Blind spots, preconceived notions, and false illusions inevitably hinder our inner development. No one achieves their best potential on their own. Outside help is always needed.

Holistic Mentoring

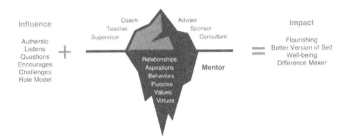

The illustration above describes what I believe is essential for a leader to become a better version of himself. It is something one grows into overtime with the assistance of an outside mentor. The term *mentor* can be defined in several ways. My intent is to be very specific in what I term "holistic mentoring." In plain terms, the holistic mentoring process is defined by this template:

Influence + Mentoring = Impact.

Influence

An effective mentor is first and foremost a person who has experienced harmony, balance, and rhythm in her own life. She knows who she is and who she is not. As a mentor, she brings a unique insight and perspective to the mentor-mentee relationship. She has good relational skills and can build trust by being open and honest. The role of the mentor is to listen, question, challenge, and encourage her mentee. The mentor serves as a role model—never perfect, but also willing to learn, change, and grow herself. Mentor-mentee relationships are not about meeting for six sessions and then out the door. The relationship is part of the life-long journey for both the mentor and mentee. The influence is mutual and reciprocal.

Mentoring

As discussed earlier, leadership is a developmental process. It is something one grows into overtime with the assistance of others. This process begins with your understanding of leadership, which we have discussed in this book, but will be summarized here to help crystalize the unique role of the mentor in this process.

Leadership is defined by your character and is based on a set of timeless and transcendent virtues—love, integrity, truth, excellence, in the context of relationships. The core of a leader is the totality of who you are and what you are about. This core serves as your inner compass, which is best measured under pressure.

This invisible core is expressed by your behavior. Your character and behavior interact with each other, each influencing the other in an ongoing dynamic. Your sense of well-being or wholeness is realized when your behavior reflects an inner life of harmony, balance, and rhythm—the best version of yourself.

The role of the mentor is to help you individually achieve this balance. The mentor cannot do this for you. This is a journey of growth that must be undertaken by each leader alone with their assistance.

There are two sides to this process: what is seen and what is unseen. Like an iceberg, what is below the waterline is what is most significant. Below the surface and at a much deeper level, the mentor works with the aspiring leader to develop and demonstrate the ability to build stronger relationships, aspirations, behaviors, purposes, and virtues over time.

The purpose of the mentor is not to provide advice or to be the expert, but to walk with you in the process: to help you see yourself clearly within a lived context at the testing point and to encourage you to incrementally level up to achieve the best version of yourself. The measure of a leader is the willingness to be held accountable to others, to learn to see yourself accurately, to assess your behaviors honestly, and work to improve continually. A leader is not someone who has arrived, but rather someone who is willing to engage with others in the process of ongoing growth, maturity, and development. To be your best you need a mentor. To achieve your best from a mentor, a leader must be open, honest, willing to change, and to be held accountable. To benefit the most from mentoring, you must be willing answer such questions as:

1. What is your story?
2. What do see as your purpose in life or life's goal?
3. What do you want people to say about you on your 80th birthday?
4. What energizes you? What drains you?
5. Share your strengths and weaknesses. What behaviors do you want to change?
6. Do you have any time bombs in your life? If you were to have a fall—publicly or privately—what would be the reason?
7. Who is the most influential person in your life? How would you rate your friendships?
8. What keeps you up at night?
9. Do you sense you are well-suited for your current work?

10. Were you raised in a family with a particular worldview? A spiritual or religious tradition?
11. What are you most afraid of?

Impact

Experience the power of harmony, balance, and rhythm. You will never forget that first time!

Of all the ways you spend your time, being mentored in your leadership has one of the highest returns on investment. The late Clayton Christensen was a distinguished Harvard Business School professor and author of *How Will You Measure Your Life?* He writes, "The only metrics that will truly matter to my life are the individuals whom I have been able to help, one by one, to become better people."

Leaders recognize that they need to be mentored because they know that the team members over which they have responsibility will need the same. We cannot be an influence on others unless we are first willing to be influenced by others. The measure of a leader is his or her willingness to be a follower first. The emerging leader will need to learn how to be mentored as well as to subsequently mentor others. It is a means by which the leader pays it forward to the next generation.

Developing the best team begins with the leader being the best team member. This is a process achieved over time, through a willingness to be vulnerable, by listening to others, encouraging them, and taking the integration of and development of virtues and relationships seriously. In short, swing in a team begins with finding swing in your life.

Chapter Thirteen

SIGNS OF A
HEALTHY ORGANIZATION

*Bobby Moch had worked out an elaborate set of
verbal codes to which only he and his crew knew
the real meanings. Some of them were simply
abbreviated versions of longer commands he
sometimes called out in the boat. 'SOS,' for
instance, meant 'slow on slides.' Most, though,
were coded because neither Moch nor his boys
wanted the other crews or the coaches to know
their exact meanings. 'WTA' meant 'wax their
ass.' 'BS' meant 'beat the sophs.' And another,
long the same lines, 'BAB' meant 'beat Al's
babies.'*

— Daniel James Brown

Moch and his oarsmen had their own secret language.
The picture of the gold medal ceremony at the 1936
Olympics has coxswain Bobby Moch standing on the top
of the podium with the other oarsmen trailing behind him
on the ground. Moch, as coxswain, the smallest of the
athletes in the winning Olympic U.S. rowing eight, never
pulled an oar. Yet he was the unquestioned leader of the
winning boat and took his place atop the medal stand.
Even more than their coach, he was the person whose
understanding they depended on and commands they
followed in the heat of the battle. The personal dynamic

he established with the oarsmen ultimately made all the difference. It is not surprising that he would later become the head crew coach at Massachusetts Institute of Technology; that he would earn a law degree from Harvard Law School and win a case in front of the U.S. Supreme Court. He was a leader.

An Olympic eight and an organization are healthy when their culture, purpose, strategy, leadership, followership fit together in an inclusive and consistent way. Are people engaged in their work or merely putting in their time? Do people trust each other? Is there a sense of purpose and enduring standard of excellence? Do they feel they are valued and are making a difference?

The leader sets the tone for the team. On one hand, an authentic leader inspires, encourages, and develops each member of the team and, in doing so, betters the team. The standards and expectations are high despite the challenges or circumstances facing the team. Team members know their backs are covered. They will have all the necessary support and will not be hung out to dry if something does not go as planned. Every person counts and is counted on.

The leader can also be toxic. Midseason when things are not going well, the culture of an NFL team always emerges most often around the character of their leader. The team's mission is vague. Roles and responsibilities are not clearly defined. There is little communication in the form of helpful feedback. Micro-management is the order of the day. Results are less than expected and one's work is reduced to merely a job. People deserve a leader who inspires, who leads by example; not one who extinguishes the life and potential of the team.

A healthy organization is one that displays:
- Clarity of purpose
- An engaged workforce
- High morale
- High retention rates
- Clear communication
- Constructive feedback, particularly when self-critical, and
- Openness to learning.

A healthy organization breeds high performance. By high performance, one looks for the ability to deliver over a prolonged period meaningful, measurable, and financially sustainable results for the people or causes the organization is in existence to serve.

Critical in a healthy organization is the dynamic of the relationships.

Some leaders mistake the relational aspect of leadership as suggesting that they engage their followers with small talk. They are not expecting this of leaders. It doesn't matter to them if you talk about sports, politics, TV shows, or the weather. They want to engage the leader in work-related conversation that enables them to grow professionally. Bestselling author Kim Scott writes, "The best way to build relationships with your team is to improve how you work together, not to take a break from working."

This demands the use of constructive feedback. It involves discussions about personal performance, strength, and areas for growth; project performance—where things went well and areas that need to be improved; overall team performance. The leader also needs to be open to feedback from the rest of the team. Where does he need to improve? How can she better support the team? Where is there a need for more resources?

Chapter Fourteen

FORGING A
DENSE NETWORK

*Those Washington crews of the 1920s and 1930s
provided an amazing number of outstanding
coaches to universities all across America. Bob
Moch distinguished himself as Washington
freshman coach, and varsity coach at MIT.
Harrison Sanford coached Cornell's 'Big Red'
crew for many years....*

*Among the other Washington oarsmen who, after
graduation, did their turns as coaches with great
distinction were Brad Raney–Columbia, Gus
Erickson–Syracuse, Loren Schoel–Marietta, Jim
McMillin–MIT, Vic Michaelson–Brown,
Charles Logg–Rutgers, Gene Melder–Clark,
Mike Murphy–Wisconsin, Dutch Schoch–
Princeton, and Ellis MacDonald–Marietta.*

— Gordon Newell

The powerful teamwork taught, demonstrated, and
experienced in the University of Washington rowing
program created a dense network of highly successful
rowing coaches. George Pocock and Al Ulbrickson
created an enduring legacy throughout the U.S. collegiate
rowing community through these other coaches. It was
not only Pocock's wooden shells that prevailed but

Pocock's rowing philosophy of teamwork that established a record of enduring success. When in 1956, George Pocock was the recipient of the Rowing Citation Award for outstanding contributions to the sport of rowing, his citation called him "probably the best-loved man in the sport of rowing." Paralleling the breath of his influence was the depth of his modesty. He is a paradigmatic exemplar of a catalytic leader of a dense network.

The social sciences are clear that the main actor on the stage of social change and influence is not the lone individual but the dense network. A person can initiate a cause, but if the cause is to make a difference, it will be because a network has been forged. A dense network is a kind of social entity that is aligned to a shared mission that is reinforced relationally that enables a cause to gain momentum and influence. Pocock's influence made rowing a national collegiate sport within the United States and broadened its area of dominance from Northeastern elite universities to all the major universities on the West coast, starting with his beloved University of Washington. Pocock's national network of influence did not begin at Harvard on the Charles River, but at Washington on Lake Washington. For years, no one took Washington and its blue-collar lumberjack oarsmen seriously. Not until they won the 1936 Berlin Olympics.

Dense networks are an influence flywheel in social change—how one makes a difference in the world. What animates dense networks are catalytic leaders. This is a leader who publicly sacrifices his own agenda for that of the team, who routinely returns authority to the team, who finds ways to empower the team without calling attention to himself while maintaining ongoing mutual accountability. When done well, the catalytic leader is increasingly replaced by a catalytic network—the team itself becomes the animating agent in the life and direction of the team, its public face. Let's unpack what this involves.

There is a common assumption that most leaders are aiming to further their own agenda, frequently through some means of coercion. This assumption must be consciously reversed if one is to be a catalytic leader in a team. The leader must demonstrate in action that their priority is the wellbeing and flourishing of the follower. Most often this demands doing something that involves the leader experiencing personal sacrifice. Sacrifice is the way in which a leader's authenticity is established and credibility restored. In a work environment, this might mean delaying a promotion, standing up for a colleague when costly, and the like. The point here is that words alone are not going to suffice; only personal costly action taken on behalf of the team will work.

Likewise, returning authority involves far more than just delegating. It means continuously considering who is the appropriate decision-maker in each situation, who will bring ownership and pride to making sure the issue is addressed effectively. The leader must selectively cede decision-making power to one's subordinates giving them permission to fail. This does not mean that the leader abdicates responsibility for the results; the buck still stops with the senior leader. But it does mean empowering one's followers so that they carry the weight of the responsibility for the decisions and actions. This is how the leader expresses trust in and for his team.

To do this effectively, the leader must provide the resources and empowerment the team needs to succeed.

Ideally, this empowerment is behind the scenes and does not cause further attention to be brought to the leader. As the team is empowered and authority returned, the leader becomes much less visible.

However, this growing invisibility is not an abandonment of ongoing mutual accountability. Two-way feedback remains necessary and mutual commitment to the results paramount.

Because these actions cannot be applied in a black and white manner, because these actions create an ongoing tension, the leader has a high degree of empathy and emotional intelligence. Leadership is a necessity for a team, but only when the team's success is the recognized priority not the leader's personal agenda. The leader must cede authority without abdicating responsibility. The leader must become increasingly invisible as the team's prominence increases, while maintaining ongoing mutual accountability. It is in the balancing of these conflicting motivations and behaviors that a catalytic leader emerges and a powerful dense network capable of lasting influence is created. The person capable of managing these tensions in a manner that creates trusts in his team is the elite leader that demonstrates high performance.

Archimedes said that if you were to give him a lever long enough and a fulcrum, he could move the world. A dense network requires a catalyst, cause, community, and context. While a dense network cannot emerge without a leader, a dense network cannot function well without a particular kind of leader. Here an effective leader must be able to connect relationally, curate ideas, and champion the cause. In doing so, he must truly believe that the team is paramount, and its flourishing is his highest priority in serving their mutual mission.

Aspiring leaders should not only look for a mentor, but also for a network of like-minded leaders who can collectively challenge them to be their best. Many leaders do not have a safe place where they can talk openly about their challenges and opportunities. When possible, leaders should join a larger network of leaders who share their passions and values and are collectively committed to one another.

George Pocock grew up in England from a long line of rivermen. Here, rowing was not a sport but a way of life, an everyday form of transportation on the Thames River. After immigrating to the Pacific Northwest, he devoted his life to the craft of making wooden boats. Over the course of his life, George was offered the head coaching job at numerous universities, all of which he refused. He knew that American rowing badly needed shells, and that if he signed up with one university, American rowing would suffer. His cause was making rowing as major a collegiate sport in America as it was in England. Through his own personal sacrifices, exemplar of character, excellence in craftmanship, and investment in the lives of his oarsmen, the George Pocock dense network changed the face of U.S. rowing forever.

Chapter Fifteen

SWING—
THE ULTIMATE
METRIC

Effective organizations can only function with effective leadership. The most effective organizations are those that form effective teams. High-performance leaders are those that can create such teams. This is evident when diverse individuals, with differing talents and personalities, are placed in situations that place them under high pressure can function sustainably in a cohesive and coordinated manner both in terms of their technical ability and emotional connectivity. This is an organization functioning with swing. In most organizations, leaders are only trained and rewarded for their mastery of technical swing, which as we have seen, is only a part of what is ultimately required for the high performance of teams.

This tall order, while doable, is rarely achieved. This failure to achieve swing is because swing is rarely the focus of the organization. Moreover, its rarely achieved because it does not easily lend itself to quantitative metrics as it is an inherently relational dynamic.

Leaders that best serve teams must have high emotional intelligence, particularly in self-regard, empathy, problem solving, interpersonal relationships, self-actualization, social responsibility, assertiveness, independence, and optimism. The other-oriented behaviors need to be grounded in the transcendent virtues of love, integrity, truth, excellence, and relationships. Finally, elite leadership can be developed, but never alone. It always necessitates a coach or mentor. A leader cannot become the best version of herself without the assistance and accountability of others.

Realizing the importance of such leaders and that organizations only become what they measure, the remaining chapters focus on the needed metrics for success; namely how to apply the vision of swing within an organization. We will look at the attitude toward change, the tensions of teamwork, and the picture of excellence.

Chapter Sixteen

CHANGE OR CHANGE

We had taken out our preliminary papers for American citizenship, and we registered for the draft of course. My name came up in the first drawing, and I was ordered to report for a pre-induction physical examination. When my turn came, the doctor noted the two missing fingers on my right hand, the result of my old injury at the Vancouver shipyard. He said, 'I guess this gets you an exemption.' I looked pleased, held out my hand and said, 'Shake, Doc.' I gave him a grip that caused him to wince a bit. It seemed that the strength of the lost fingers had gone into the others; an instance of nature compensating. I laughed and told him I didn't want an exemption, and he agreed I didn't seem to need one after all.

— George Pocock

With the war effort ramping up, collegiate rowing was in limbo. Pocock and his crew had been hired to work for the Boeing Airplane Company to make wooden pontoons for seaplanes. Days after Pocock's induction physical, General Crowder, head of the national draft, visited the Boeing shop. After watching Pocock work for a few minutes, the General said, "I see you are to go and prepare to fight the Germans." Pocock answered, "Sir, I will be proud to go." The General replied, "No you will not! You can be of far more use to the war effort right where you are." As such Pocock's career pivoted to making wooden Curtiss H.S.-2 flying boats.

As World War I came to an end, the Boeing orders were cut in half. With time on their hands, Pocock's team built two racing shells in the large Boeing hanger. Ironically, it was these two racing shells that launched Boeing back into the airplane business. A Congressional committee from Washington was reviewing wartime aircraft plants to determine if they were worthy of further government contracts.

There in the empty Boeing hanger lay the gleaming sixty feet long new shells. One member of the committee reviewed them closely, "Who on earth built these? I rowed at Harvard, and I never expected to see anything like this out here. I would like to meet the builders and talk to them." Edgar Gott, the general manager of the plant added, "That's the kind of workmen we have here." Shortly afterward, Boeing received orders for 200 pursuit planes. The company has never looked back since. Pivoting to building planes from racing shells, Pocock's winning philosophy translated to a new opportunity.

Change in an organization is inevitable. What differs between organizations is how they understand and implement corporate change. Building on the work of Edgar and Peter Schein's *The Corporate Culture Survival Guide,* John Kotter's *Leading Change,* Clayton Christensen's "The Tools of Cooperation and Change," as well as my own personal experience, we have developed the Severn Leadership Group Organizational Change Model. Two things become self-evident in this model. First, organizations must learn to adapt to change.

Second, managing the inevitability of change within a team or organization places a special demand on its leader as change often engenders fear and a decrease in trust.

Organizational Change Model

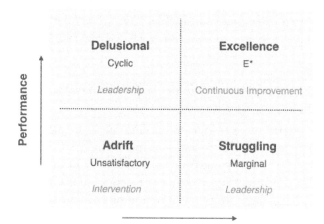

Fearless Reviews, Desire Improvement

Horizontal Axis

The horizontal axis of Fearless Reviews and Desire Improvement represents the degree to which an organization will look critically at its performance, people, processes, and its commitment to their purpose/mission. The organization does not fear what they will learn when performance reviews are conducted. They have an inherent desire for continuous improvement. This axis is about the organization's willingness to change and move toward excellence.

Vertical Axis

This axis is the metric of the overall performance of the organization. It is the degree to which the mission/purpose is being fulfilled. Several indicators can assess this performance, depending on the organization and its size. This axis represents the actual performance of the organization moving toward excellence. The results of these two axes creates quadrants that are similar to the Individual Change model, which we discussed earlier.

Adrift
(No fearless reviews and minimum desire to improve with unsatisfactory performance)

This organization's long-term outlook is bleak. Poor morale, low standards and unsatisfactory performance characterize this organization with little hope or desire for change. Meaningful performance metrics are not evident or used. The organization is functioning without a rudder and compass and are thus in the doldrums adrift. An outside organizational intervention is required.

Someone must step in and create a *sense of urgency*. She must be direct and to the point. The organization must face the facts about its performance and own it. Either it changes or it will not survive as is. It is a tough message, but it must be communicated. For some, it will have been a long time in coming. Others would rather leave than change. The message is simply, "Change or change"— change the way we work or change where you work.

It is important for the leader to assemble a specific team to guide the change process. Kotter writes, "This is a powerful group – guiding the change – one with leadership skills, credibility, communication skills, authority, analytic skills, and a sense of urgency." To the degree that outsiders are brought in to be a part of this team, which is often necessary, it increases the challenge of establishing the necessary dynamics of trust.

The leader must be authentic and exhibit the core behaviors of love, integrity, truth, excellence, and relationships, and be fully committed to her people and her organization. This is essential for developing healthy relationships and creating increased levels of trust. This gets the change process underway.

Struggling
(Fearless reviews and desire to improve with poor performance)

This organization has the potential to recover. It wants change, but it does not know how, nor has a clear sense of what excellence looks like. A good place to begin in this situation is for the leader and key influencers in the organization to review thoroughly performance data. Ask why performance is as it is. Dig into the details and look for trends. The results could be quite revealing for everyone.

The leader must establish a well communicated and understood vision and strategy, empower others to act, develop teamwork, encourage teamwork, standardize policies and procedures, seek short-term wins, and perhaps consider the infusion of a few select new people from the outside. This is difficult and often frustrating work, but there are no shortcuts. Building a new team, setting the standards and expectations, and developing a high level of trust takes time. All this work will pay huge dividends in the end.

Delusional
(No fearless reviews and minimum desire to improve with high performance)

This is perhaps the most difficult organization to tackle. Their overall performance is excellent, but it is not sustainable. Somewhere, over time, they have lost their ability to be self-reflective. Cracks in their performance go unnoticed. Complacency sets in and performance begins to either ebb or stagnate, as other organizations around them continue to improve and set new standards for performance. A downturn in performance metrics is ignored or considered momentary. When an entire industry is facing external threats, these become changes that are impossible to ignore.

The Leader

Technical Competence	Capability but at a cost	E* Capability for sustained *Excellence*
	Failure	Limited Capability

Organizational Expertise

A second version of this quadrant is that a forceful leader has driven the performance to high levels. From the outside looking in, many would classify the organization as a top performer. The leadership team in this case is a one-man-band. When this leader departs, organizational performance drops and the rest of the organization collapses—worn out and not prepared to forge ahead on their own.

In the first case, the organization is delusional in the sense that they believe having reached the top, their journey is complete. "We will just keep doing what we are doing today, and we will do just fine"—until tomorrow!

In the second case, the one-man-band is in a state of delusion. He views himself as an effective leader. "Look at my performance!" Unfortunately, when you look at what he leaves behind, there is a trail of untapped potential, missed opportunities for team development, and collapsing performance.

In this quadrant, the leader must lead by example, exhibiting the core virtues/behaviors (LITER) day in and day out. The core of the organization needs to be restored. This begins by listening, building relationships and trust, watching, questioning, encouraging, challenging, communicating, setting clear standards, developing new teams, and restoring the organization's understanding of what is needed and what is possible. For organizations still performing well, there will be resistance to this change at first. The long-term view must be encouraged over short-term thinking and metrics.

Excellence or E*

(Fearless reviews and desired improvement = excellent performance)

This organization has the capacity for sustained excellence across the board and over time. Though their performance will have normal fluctuations, they are able to make improvements and learn from their experiences.

There is a high level of trust throughout the organization. Everyone knows their role and responsibilities. They feel accountable for their actions, responsible for each other, and are focused on mission success, organizational improvement, and personal growth. This team is fully engaged.

The leader has developed solid technical competence and organizational expertise within herself, as well as those within her organization. She is authentic, knows her strengths and weaknesses, and recognizes that excellence begins with her own behavior and actions.

The key to staying in this quadrant is to be open to critical feedback both from internal and external sources and never become complacent. This organization understands the difference between success and excellence. They know when to celebrate and when it is time to move on.

No two organizational change transformations are identical, but the fundamentals required by each remain the same. If we are to be leaders of change, leaders of transformation, we must understand the challenges and opportunities involved in moving a team toward organizational excellence. Leading change takes courage, commitment, and a sense of personal well-being. An organization can change only to the degree its leadership will change. Here a leader's personal virtues/behaviors will clearly be put to the test. Leading change with courage by sacrificing time, attention, and training to love team members is very effective. Integrity is key to seeing what is truly happening and resolve conflicts among the team. Speaking truth can motivate change and build relationships with customers and the team. Excellence can drive change and can make the future attractive. Finally, relationships become even more essential in times of change to unify leaders and the team, to bring partners in to support the change, and to co-opt customers in the future. It is here where the strength of a leader's virtues is most tested.

The Dynamics of Accepting Change

The second model relevant to this discussion on the requirements of a leader facilitating organizational change is the response curve. This is adapted from a model originally developed by Elizabeth Kubler-Ross in the 1960s to explain the grieving process and accepting the inevitability of death and dying. Since then, it has been used and adapted by many as a method of helping people understand their reactions to significant change. This blended version of the model and discussion has four basic stages: denial, resistance, exploration, and commitment.

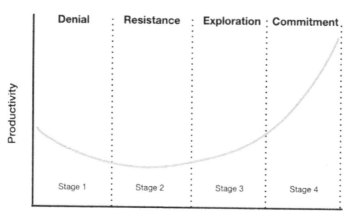

Denial (Stage 1)

In the denial stage, the organization experiences shock. The first question is, "Why do we have to change?" The status quo is assumed to be just fine. People often feel threatened. People are fearful of the unknown.

> *What you see*: indifference, disbelief, and avoidance
> *What you hear*: silence, it will never happen, it won't affect me
> *Approach*: listen and communicate what you know and can share often

Resistance (Stage 2)

As the shock wears off, resistance sets in. Often the blame game begins—finding someone else or something else to blame. There is great suspicion and frustration. Morale sinks. At this point resistance bottoms out. As people accept that change is genuine, apathy or remoteness sets in.

> *What you see:* anger, complaining, glorifying the past, skepticism, unwillingness to take part
> *What you hear:* it won't work, it used to be, the data is flawed
> *Approach:* watch, listen, acknowledge, validate, support

Exploration (Stage 3)

As the darker emotions of Stage 2 subside, a more optimistic mode emerges. People accept the fact that change is inevitable. They think about new opportunities; new goals; necessary training; how to best be organized. One must encourage this exploration to be about the organization rather than the individual, who may take this opportunity to look for new work elsewhere. This stage raises many questions and the need for thoughtful answers. Hope and trust are on the rise.

> *What you see*: energy, risk-taking tentativeness, impatience, activity without focus
> *What you hear*: optimism, I have an idea, let's try, what if?
> *Approach*: give time to explore and test, develop capability, celebrate small wins

Commitment (Stage 4)

Exploration turns to commitment. Development plans are made. Additional responsibilities and specific tasks are put into place. There is a greater sense of energy and enthusiasm. People want to move on and get the change behind them. Organizational loyalty increases.

> *What you see*: future orientation, initiative, confidence
> *What you hear:* how can I contribute, let's get on with it
> *Approach:* celebrate and commend

This model is useful for both individuals and groups. The speed that people and groups move through each stage varies. Some will be quicker than others. If people do not adequately feel heard and supported, then they may even move backward. This process is not always toward a positive resolution, reversals are possible.

Leaders must appreciate the change process and understand what state the organization is always in. This means that anticipated change must be carefully planned and communicated at every level. Rarely does ramming a change through work. The need for change may be very clear, but individuals and organizations need to feel appreciated and supported throughout all the inevitable changes. Sensitivity to the process is key.

The winds of change are never going away. This is more pronounced today than ever before. The average worker is expected to change their careers twelve times over the course of their lives. Organizations that have long been resistant to change are the very ones most likely to experience the most abrupt and cataclysmic change. The question of how one leads an organization through change has become increasingly important. There is no magic process or guarantee of success. But the inevitability of change establishes the environment in which both leaders and followers will be most tested. The difference makers in this situation are:

- A diverse group of men and women
- Who live with a strong sense of purpose
- Who exhibit strong character, behavior anchored by a set of timeless and transcendent virtues
- Who appreciate that life is ultimately about relationships and people
- Who leverage today's challenges for a flourishing tomorrow
- Who listen, learn, and act
- Who know they need others and create a team
- Who are people of courage and hope
- Who live consciously between what is and what can be, and
- Who are authentic.

When Pocock pivoted his career from building rowing shells to airplane pontoons, he could blame the war effort for the inevitability. But it was his acceptance of the change, reestablishing his team at Boeing, and maintenance of high standards that set his leadership apart. We tend to tell the stories of great men as random snapshots rather than as moving pictures. Pocock was eventually able to return to his first love of building rowing shells, eventually establishing the company Pocock Racing Shells. Decades later, the emphasis on excellence in teamwork and network is evidenced in the company. The power of team still stands out. They write on their website,

> While some boat builders try to tell you that the boat makes a difference, we know that cultures of excellence are created by athletes, coaches, and their support networks. It is the hard work and teamwork of these stakeholders that win races and create positive and transformative boathouse environments.
>
> When you bring a Pocock Racing Shell into your boathouse, the Pocock Team becomes part of your support network, upholding and supporting the standard of excellence required for success in our sport.

Can one maintain the power of a team under the inevitable conditions of change? These conditions are varied. In the end, change may be the organization's greatest challenge and competitor.

Chapter Seventeen

MANAGING THE TENSIONS OF TEAMWORK

There was one more thing about cedar—a sort of secret that Pocock had discovered accidentally after his first shells made of the wood had been in the water for a while.... Once they were exposed to water both their bows and sterns tended to curve ever so slightly upward... Because the cedar was dry when attached to the frame but then became wet after being used regularly, the wood wanted to expand slightly in length. However, the interior frame of the boat, being made of ash that remained perpetually dry and rigid, would not allow it to expand. The cedar skin thus became compressed, forcing the ends of the boat up slightly and lending it what boatbuilders called 'camber.' The result was that the boat as a whole was under subtle but continual tension like a drawn bow waiting to be released. This gave it a kind of liveliness, a tendency to spring forward on the catch of the oars in a way that no other design or material could duplicate.

— Daniel James Brown

A Pocock wooden shell was built to be under continuous tension. Its performance success was tied to this tension. So too are successful organizations. It is never just one thing that matters for high performance, but multiple factors, often conflicting, that must be held in ongoing dynamic tension. Organizational excellence demands a systems-based perspective placed in constructive tension managed by an emotionally healthy leader of good character.

What are the key factors that must be kept in tension?

The first element is that of leadership. It is paramount to achieving organizational excellence. A leader's character, behavior, humility, selfless courage, and commitment to serve others above self must be resolute. *Leadership makes or breaks an organization.* Too often the leader is the barrier to releasing the skills, abilities, ideas, and potential of others in the organization. The decision to embrace these qualities in others and release this resourcefulness starts with the leader and then must trickle down throughout the organization.

The second key element of organizational performance is technical competence. It is having the appropriate level of knowledge, technical proficiency, skill, experience, and training for one's profession. It is safe to say that most organizations place a heavy emphasis on this element to the neglect of the other needed elements. Many organizations bias the mechanical over the relational, the impersonal over the personal to their own loss. The emphasis on swing is an antidote to this tendency.

The third key element is organizational expertise. It is having both an understanding of organizational dynamics, and the compassion and behaviors to develop and encourage the best in people. The evidence of this element is trust. When a leader can inspire people and mold them into a team, they develop trust. When this occurs, they have set the conditions for further development and success. Trust engenders confidence, commitment, and an organizational culture that is unbeatable. It is this dimension that is typically the most lacking in an organization coupled with the failure of leadership to make this a high priority. Leadership, technical competence, and organizational expertise are the three key elements of organizational performance.

An excellent organization is one where there is high technical competence and high organizational expertise. The key measure here is sustained excellence as all organizations will go through normal fluctuations. The question is whether they can learn from their mistakes and experience. An elite leader is the person who can build a team that functions over time with a high degree of trust.

There is no one, secret recipe for creating a high-performance team. It demands a holistic approach that keeps multiple things in constant and evolving tension. To do this, a leader needs a high level of emotional intelligence. Jennifer Jordan, Michael Wade, Elizabeth Teracino in *Harvard Business Review* suggest that an effective leader must simultaneously balance seven tensions.

1. The Expert vs. the Learner – here, technical competence needs to be balanced with relational humility. A leader must be willing to learn from others.
2. The Constant vs. the Adaptor – here, leaders must recognize that they are working in fast-changing environments and must be always willing to challenge the status quo.
3. The Tactician vs. the Visionary – here, the visionary leader must be constantly grounded in

a concrete roadmap as to how to achieve it. Reality must be constantly tested.

4. The Teller vs. the Listener – here, the leader must value listening carefully to others before making decisions. This must be balanced with the leader's experience, ability, and viewpoint.

5. The Power Holder vs. The Power Sharer – here, the balance between returning authority to others and retaining authority must be balanced depending on the context of the decision and the expertise of those involved.

6. The Intuitionist vs. the Analyst – here, going with one's gut must be balanced with the slower approach of receiving and assessing analytic data. There are certainly times when there is no time to wait for more data and when the data cannot take into consideration all the nuances that the decision demands.

7. The Perfectionist vs. the Accelerator – here, the need for the best can get in the way of good. Many key decisions must be made before perfection can be achieved, and yet hasty decisions without ample consideration can also lead to bad results.

Effective leaders cannot rigidly adopt one approach over the other. Rather, they need the ability to be ambidextrous depending on the context and people involved. To achieve this balance, the leader needs emotional intelligence and systems in place that foster feedback and build trust. Because people are the key, leadership in an organization cannot be approached in a mechanistic style or without a team approach. Effective leadership embraces these tensions.

People want to make a difference. People want to work within a high performing team. They want to be fully engaged in their work. They want leaders who strive for excellence. The winning edge in a racing shell is the same as that for every organization, the people in the boat. Make no mistake about it, developing an E* organization is challenging and often messy work. It takes time and dedication. Creating swing within an organization is the task and responsibility of every leader. It is an experience when achieved that few will ever forget. Pocock made this clear when he stated, "When you get the rhythm in an eight, it's pure pleasure to be in it. It's easy work when the rhythm comes—that is 'swing' as they call it. I've heard men shriek out with delight when the swing came in an eight; it's a thing they'll never forget as long as they live."

To this end, let's drill down further on the word excellence. It is important to understand that excellence is not a synonym for perfection or for success. It can't be reduced to simply winning. Excellence is as much about how things are done as the results of the effort. Excellence is:

1. An innate and unrelenting passion within a person or an organization to continually:
    o Pursue continual improvement, always building upon yesterday's achievements
    o Build personal relationships and organizational mastery
    o Admit and learn from failures
    o Seek better practices and processes
    o Develop integrated and cohesive teamwork and support
    o Setting high standards, holding people accountable

- o Not being satisfied with today's performance or results
- o Learn from both success and failure
2. Not about self or looking good, but about the sustained pursuit of a worthy goal, a mission, a purpose
3. Not the endpoint of a race, but the journey of learning and growing to get there.

The journey of excellence leads to sustained, exemplary levels of performance. The evidence is quite clear. Organizations with a sustained pursuit of excellence have an engaged and highly motivated workforce, high levels of trust, well integrated teams, better outcomes, and a better bottom line economically, socially, and environmentally.

The journey of excellence is never complete. There are always new opportunities and challenges. If the purpose is big and audacious, then it must be something we cannot do alone. Others are needed for their expertise, wisdom, encouragement, and willingness to roll up their sleeves and work. When one stumbles, another can pick him up. When there is success, all can celebrate. When there is failure, all can learn and grow. The team is in it together for the long haul.

The measure of an elite leader is her ability to manage organizational tension by creating sustained technical and relational swing within an organization. There has been much that has been written about leadership. In the end, leadership is not about the leader at all, but the team and the performance of the team under pressure over time.

Such leaders are rare because such leaders are not developed. It is my belief and experience that every leader can move closer to being such a leader beginning with a personal commitment, developing behavioral practices, maintaining ongoing accountability while dealing with the actual complexities of an organization. Leadership is never really learned in a vacuum, through a book, or in an MBA program. It is only learned in practice during an actual race with an actual team and accountability partner. Such leaders are elite, not because they are inherently special, but because they inevitably make a lasting difference. They are the difference makers.

Chapter Eighteen

EXCELLENCE: REACHING FOR THE STARS

Joe, when you really start trusting those other boys, you will feel a power at work within you that is far beyond anything you have ever imagined. Sometimes you will feel as if you have rowed right off the planet and are rowing among the stars.

— George Pocock

Organizations become what they measure. What they measure reflects their priorities. Yet not everything that counts can be easily counted. Sometimes the best coaching comes by feel, by observing every detail of each aspect of the stroke in each oarsman over time. Knowing what to look for is key and this is an art learned over time in the coach's launch.

The concept of swing retains this mysterious ineffability. It is an experienced reality that is just beyond the easily describable. To get at it, an organization's attitude toward change is critical, maintaining the necessary tensions of teamwork necessary, and having a clear shared picture of excellence foundational. This picture must be held in common with all the team members, embodied by the leader, and then choreographed by the leader. It is only the coach or leader who has the distanced perspective to constantly observe the whole. As such, the final accountability for achieving swing is with the leader.

Excellence is swing. It is not an act or an endpoint. It is a desire to learn, and to grow. It is a process of unremitting improvement, continually seeking to reach for the stars. It is only in that journey that we can feel whole. A number of years ago the chairman of a large corporation inquired, "Almost all of my businesses are doing well. I have spent a lot of money getting them there. Is it possible for all of these businesses to go from above-average to excellent?" His corporation was technically competent, but for the most part, the people-side of the business had been neglected. There were a lot of bodies strewn along the highway to that above-average performance. A leader can drive performance... but only for so long. The time will come when the team's performance declines and people are burned out.

An excellent organization, one that achieves sustained excellence, is composed of teams, unified by a common set of core virtues and behaviors, a common purpose, and an unwavering commitment to reach for the stars. It always starts with the leader. You set the tone, the atmosphere for development, growth, and performance. Your integrity and authenticity are measured by your actual behavior.

Leadership begins with you being:
- A person of character and committed to a life that is not about self but serving others
- A person with a strong sense of self—who is authentic and self-aware recognizing her

strengths and weaknesses—while desiring to learn and grow
- A person with a passion for the mission and cause
- A person who listens, questions, challenges, and encourages
- A person who holds himself and others accountable
- A builder of relationships that foster the development of excellent teams
- A person who displays empathy, who seeks to understand others when their experiences and perspectives are distinctly different from her own, and
- A person focused on building teams and not her own career.
- A person with appropriate technical expertise.

Leadership begins with you, but is not about you. Your commitment to your followers must be unwavering. This is manifested by:
- Communicating a clear vision/purpose
- Knowing your people
  o What is important to them
  o What are their dreams and concerns
  o Their strengths and needed areas for growth
  o What is needed for them to be successful
- Building their skills and abilities
  o Ensure the basics
  o Professional mastery
  o Personal development
- Setting standards of excellence
  o Holding people accountable

- o Each person knows and owns their area of responsibility
- o Developing standardized administrative and work processes
- Providing constructive feedback
  - o Publicly and privately saying thank you
- Seeking their input and feedback
  - o Processes and practices that can be improved or removed
  - o What is going well and what is not
  - o How you can help team performance

It is only when these matters are aggressively pursued, as a starting point, that the leader's technical competence comes into play.

Jamie Dimon, Chairman and CEO of J.P. Morgan Chase, cautions his people that one of the major derailers of performance is when an organization forgets its A-B-Cs. These three must be avoided at all costs.

A – Arrogance   B – Bureaucracy   C – Complacency

Any or all the A-B-Cs erode an organization's ability to learn, innovate, and grow. They are organizational killers. You must learn to recognize and eliminate them.

The final aspect of a leader is his ability to provide organizational expertise. This expertise involves the ability to implement these factors in specific organizational situations made up of particular and diverse individuals seeking to achieve a common goal under pressure. It is here that the holistic synergy of leadership is seen.

Make no mistake, the key drivers of organizational performance are its people, team cohesion, working relationships, and overall results/outcomes. Each of these can be developed, prioritized, measured, and assessed. When these aspects are periodically evaluated, a clear picture of overall performance will emerge. When compared to that of an E* team, you will recognize your strengths and areas for improvement. This ongoing pursuit of excellence is a sign of a high-performance team at work.

There are no excellent teams without an excellent leader. Excellence of this nature spreads from the leader throughout the entire organization. People want to be on a team with a trusted and respected leader, an engaged workforce, high morale, and superior results. E* leaders create E* teams, which fosters E* organizations. This means that the more senior the leader, the more that leader's performance evaluation as a leader, should be based solely on her success in creating an effective team. The ability to build a high-performance team is the ultimate measure of an effective leader.

Finally, it should be reinforced that this is not a static checklist, but an ongoing process that can only be developed from experience over time and experience that includes crises and failure. A book can only point as a guide. It is experience that makes it real and gets leadership squarely into the bones of an individual. Leaders are not born. They are made during the daily grind. Their leadership abilities are then revealed in moments of intense competition and crisis. When this kind of leader spills over on the entire team, the team is then set up for the experience of swing. Swing is not an accident, but the culmination of a host of variables coming into perfect harmony. It's no wonder that when achieved "you will feel as if you have rowed right off the planet and are rowing among the stars."

Conclusion

THE CALLING OF DIFFERENCE MAKERS

George Yeoman Pocock died at Seattle on March
19, 1976, four days short of his eighty-fifth
birthday.... The closing words of the memorial
services at the University Christian Church
were, fittingly, his rowing creed—
> *It's a great art, is rowing,*
> *It's the finest art there is.*
> *It's a symphony of motion.*
> *And when you're rowing well*
> *Why it's nearing perfection—*
> *And when you reach perfection*
> *You're touching the Divine,*
> *It touches the you of you's*
> *Which is your soul.*

— Gordon Newell and Dick Erickson

The accomplishments that matter the most in a life well-lived, are relational experiences with others. A meaningful accomplishment of a team is a memory that time does not fade. Aging oarsmen and battle-scarred soldiers return for their reunions. The intensity of the comradeship forged in competition or on the battlefield never fades. When you have "touched the Divine" together it touches the depths of your soul.

159

There is a special meaning that comes to life when one lives a life of selfless courage in service to noble ends with others on a team. A team accomplishment far outweighs individual accomplishment. It is greater because it is far more difficult to achieve. It is greater because it has a far wider and lasting impact. It is greater because it expands the significance of meaning. It is greater because it most closely resembles the collaborative ecosystem of nature. It is greater because it effectively reflects the Divine.

Leaders are made, not born. There are leaders who can accomplish a task. And then there are leaders who can accomplish a task through a team. Within all organizations, these are the elite leaders. These are the curators of swing, the makers of meaning, and the magicians of the soul. It is to these leaders that this book is dedicated for these are the ultimate difference makers.

Organizations become what they measure. The most important thing to measure in an organization is the most difficult thing to measure. Nonetheless, this does not make it any less real. Organizations need to aspire to and measure the ineffable experience of swing in their teams. Here, I have only suggested some of the components of swing. There is no fixed recipe or formula because every situation is different, and every team is composed of different kinds of people. Nonetheless, organizations will not achieve swing unless they aspire to swing. This may require putting down the spreadsheet and picking up a book of poetry. They may require highlighting the soft skills of empathy and listening. This demands holistic relational thinking. It changes the priorities of an organization. It demands placing the team above the individual. Swing is the haunted longing of every employee. Every team member longs for the additive experience of flow with others toward a shared goal of noble accomplishment. That swing is rare, only serves to make its achievement more valuable. Swing is the collective experience to which all high-performing teams aspire. Swing is the balance of character and behavior in service to emotional intelligence in every team member. Swing in a team is the true measure of an elite high performing leader. Swing is relational poetry under pressure; the ballet forged in pain.

About the Author

Sigval (Sig) M. Berg is the founder and current chairman of the board of The Severn Leadership Group in Annapolis, Maryland. A distinguished graduate of the U.S. Naval Academy, he served as the chief engineer on the nuclear-powered submarine USS Sunfish (SSN649). He completed the Harvard Graduate School of Business' Advanced Management Program and has a MDIV from Trinity Lutheran Seminary. He was an Executive Vice President at the Institute of Nuclear Power Operations and Managing Director of the World Association of Nuclear Operators in London and the Senior Vice President for Infrastructure Development and Training at UniStar Nuclear Energy. He also served as a senior pastor at Good Shepherd Church in Naperville, Illinois over a congregation of nearly 1,000 members. He and his wife, Martha, live in Annapolis, Maryland. He has three daughters and six grandchildren.

About Severn Leadership Group

The Severn Leadership Group trains, mentors, and networks elite leaders to serve in effective teams. The firm's distinguishing emphasis is on the power of effective teams and the unique characteristics of leadership needed to create such teams. For over a decade, it has seeded emotionally healthy selfless leaders in service of the greater good to positions within government and institutions of global importance.

More information about The Severn Leadership Groups' Fellows Program can be found at
https://severnleadership.org/programs/fellows-program

Made in United States
Orlando, FL
07 June 2022

18595951R00089